UNDERST...

THE

GRAND DESIGN

SPIRITUAL REALITY'S INNER LOGIC

by

Joachim E. Wolf

Printed in Victoria, Canada

National Library of Canada Cataloguing in Publication Data

Wolf, Joachim, 1927-
     Understanding the grand design : spiritual reality's inner logic /
Joachim Wolf.
Includes bibliographical references and index.
ISBN 1-55395-567-6
     1. Religion and science. 2. Spiritual life. I.
Title.
BL240.3.W64 2003   291.1'75   C2003-900210-1

TRAFFORD

This book was published *on-demand* in cooperation with Trafford Publishing. On-demand publishing is a unique process and service of making a book available for retail sale to the public taking advantage of on-demand manufacturing and Internet marketing. **On-demand publishing** includes promotions, retail sales, manufacturing, order fulfilment, accounting and collecting royalties on behalf of the author.

Suite 6E, 2333 Government St., Victoria, B.C. V8T 4P4, CANADA
Phone   250-383-6864   Toll-free   1-888-232-4444 (Canada & US)
Fax   250-383-6804   E-mail   sales@trafford.com
Web site   www.trafford.com   TRAFFORD PUBLISHING IS A DIVISION OF TRAFFORD
HOLDINGS LTD.
Trafford Catalogue #02-1283   www.trafford.com/robots/02-1283.html

10   9   8   7   6   5   4   3

Contents

ACKNOWLEDGEMENTS

My heartfelt thanks go to my dear family members and friends who have helped me to create this book. My daughters Carol and Karen have contributed much through their editing efforts and their valuable suggestions. Carol carried most of the workload, diligently editing several drafts, eliminating my "German accent", and asking penetrating questions about the book's content. Her participation resulted in a number of important improvements. Throughout this effort, my dear wife, Erika, provided valuable suggestions and patiently accepted the fact that I spent long hours to work in my office. Ronald, my son-in-law, energetically applied his computer expertise to rescue me from a number of software problems. I also very much appreciate the detailed, thoughtful, and constructive comments from our good friend Steffie Mazzeo-Caputo. Finally, I want to thank all of those who helped me to become the person I am today. They have contributed to my ability to write this book.

INTRODUCTION

This book is a labor of love. I hope that it will help you experience joy, peace and satisfaction as I do. It is a story of finding answers to age-old questions such as:

What is life all about?
How should we live.
How can we come out on top?
What is the top?

I asked these questions when I finally made it back to my home city Berlin after the end of World War II. I was twenty years old then and attempting to bring some direction and normalcy into my life after the turbulent experiences of the war. I would like to tell you how my struggle to cope with the events of that time started me on a mental odyssey that eventually brought me "heaven on earth."

When I arrived, I was appalled how Berlin, once Germany's proud capital, was utterly devastated. Berlin's condition was symbolic of the state of our whole nation and of the political system that had governed it. The surviving citizens had begun to dig out from under the rubble. Food was even more scarce than it had been before the end of the war. People bartered their personal belongings for food on the black market. Those who had lost everything were utterly desperate and many didn't survive.

I had lost several family members and the rest were scattered throughout the country. Only my uncle and an aunt were still in Berlin, struggling to survive. My home had been confiscated by the authorities and was now crowded with three displaced families. Living space was extremely scarce since most buildings were destroyed. But I was lucky to have found a room for rent. Its windows were shattered and I covered them up with cardboard. Somehow I acquired a little stove, a necessity since the central heating system did not work. There was a tiny balcony, and from it I could look down onto the ruins and into the streets beyond.

My first priority was to survive. I had had some experience in electronics, so I found a job as a technician in the Blaupunkt Werke radio company that had recently reopened. My next priority was to finish my high school education, which had been interrupted during the war. At age fifteen I had been drafted, along with my classmates, as "Luftwaffenhelfer" (Air Force Helper). Originally we were called "Young-Soldiers" and we were proud of this label. However, the induction of child soldiers caused an international outrage, so the Government changed our titles, but not our assignments.

We operated the anti-aircraft (Flak) batteries that defended Berlin. I actually welcomed this arrangement. My mother had died a few weeks earlier, and my father did not have to worry about what to do with me after my call to duty. He had been somewhat aloof with his two sons and it was clear that he was in over his head. Besides, I did not enjoy my assignment as a homemaker, even though it gave me a chance to hone my cooking skills by flipping pancakes at the ceiling. The occasional pancake landed on the floor and my father and brother wondered what tasted so gritty between their teeth.

During our duty as anti-aircraft operators, we continued our high school education in the mornings, trained on the Flak equipment until supper, did our homework in the evenings, and defended Berlin against air raids during the night. Whenever a raid lasted beyond midnight, we did not go to school the next morning. Eventually we were transferred to regular military service without having finished high school. Defending the Fatherland had become more important.

Now, after I had gained a foothold in West Berlin, I went back to school in the mornings and cut my work load (and earnings) in half at Blaupunkt Werke. It was tough. I was alone, and I didn't have enough to eat. Often, I ground a potato into boiling water, added salt and some spice, and had a pot full of thick pulp that gave me the illusion of having had enough to eat. Some days I couldn't go to school and work because I was too exhausted. Despite it all, I overcame my difficulties and received my high school diploma.

As hard as this time was, it was nevertheless invigorating. I drew on my innermost reserves and this put me in touch with the essence of life that is in all of us. I felt a certain high and – this may sound strange – I had the distinct feeling of having been helped and protected. I was not religious, although I had received Lutheran training and had been confirmed at age fourteen. But I did not believe in Jesus Christ, or in angels. However, I had the peculiar sensation that invisible entities were looking after me.

A high school course in philosophy had motivated me to think about the deeper issues of life, and given the destruction of the world in which I had grown up, I wanted to understand the meaning of it all. I felt that I had been used and lied to. After all that had happened, what or whom in the world could I trust? I wondered what the basis of my life should be. I wanted to find out for myself what life was about. As a result, I started to spend most of my spare time pondering this question. The more I thought about it, the more important it became for me to find an answer and the more I focused on my search. My quest became an obsession. Eventually I boiled it down to one key question: do I have free will in the face of the overwhelming circumstances that had devastated this city, indeed the whole nation? Was I master of my own destiny, or was some unknown higher force determining my fate? Was I only a pawn that was being pushed around in a big chess game that I did not understand?

To find the answer, I toyed with various thought-experiments, imagining the moments that define us and how we might, or should, react. And then, the answer was there, accompanied by an overwhelming feeling of freedom, joy and certainty. I "saw" a single entity, a super-being, comprised of individuals that were united in the way that our physical body unites the individual organs. I perceived two levels of reality, the physical one of individuals, and superimposed upon them, a group-entity that was much more powerful than the individuals themselves, though they were not aware of this greater entity. The group-entity existed as a distinct being at its own level of reality. With this insight came a deep intuitive understanding of the intimate give-and-take relationship between the group-entity and the individuals that belonged to it. This vision was so clear that its truth was beyond any doubt in my mind.

Here was the answer to the question, are we free or are our actions determined by a higher power? I sensed that individuals are part of a higher force, their group-entity. However I understood that each one is still free to follow his own will, because his will and the will of the group-entity are the same. From the individual's viewpoint, the group-entity is in his heart, in his soul. Actually, the group entity *is* the common soul of all individuals. Therefore each person instinctively **wants** to do what the higher entity of his group wants. And he who can do what he wants is free. Soon this vision spread into my daily life. I realized that we, as human beings, are related members of a group-entity that is much larger and more powerful than we can imagine. We can't see it, yet it is very real inside all of us. This group entity defines us as humans, and we express our unity with it when we speak from our hearts.

Within a few days, a logical concept of greater reality fell into place naturally and easily in my mind: ultimately, there had to be a supreme Group-Entity for the entire universe, transcending, encompassing and permeating all that exists. This Entity was also the innermost essence of everyone and everything, including me. I realized that this must be what we call God. I had heard this before, but now I understood that God was inside me, right there and then, in my heart. This realization suddenly swept me away into another state of consciousness. I can't find words to describe this experience. It was heaven. I was engulfed in a bliss of mutual love with the ultimate source of the universe. It was very powerful then, and the thought of it is still quite emotional now.

After my euphoric experience I hurried to explain my newfound understanding to my friends, but I couldn't find the right words. The words simply didn't exist. My friends listened politely, but they obviously didn't understand what I was talking about. I tried to make it sound plausible by using physical analogies, but this turned out to be more comical than inspiring. Yet I knew that I had been exposed to an enlightening experience that would change my whole life. I decided then that I would devote my life to living according to the truth that I had witnessed. I knew that there was a higher, more advanced, reality beyond our life of suffering and warfare. While I was having my enlightening experience, lying on the couch in my room, I sensed the ruins outside and the troubled people as a hazy illusion, and I felt compelled to shout to them not to despair, that everything was actually all right. But they would not have understood. They would have thought that I was crazy.

So I decided to pursue my new belief, to test these insights as I went about the tasks of my daily life. After all, I had been willing to give up my life for my country, fighting for a cause that had turned out to be contemptible. Now I was aware of a much nobler cause and I was willing to lay my life on the line for it. I wanted to live my truth until I could communicate it to others.

In 1991 I wrote a paper titled *Revolution in Common Sense,* outlining the basic concepts of how we can understand true reality by moving beyond our present concepts. I distributed the paper to a select group of scientists and published it in 1994 on the Internet through CompuServe. Since December 1996 it can be accessed on my website *Quantum Metaphysics*[1]. I have received many requests to write more about this subject using less "scientific" language. I hope that this book will satisfy this call.

---

[1] http://home.sprynet.com/~jowolf

PART 1

THE BASICS

Chapter 1

The Invisible Reality

NEW DIMENSIONS

Some 2400 years ago, Plato taught us that we do not see the world as it really is. In his famous cave allegory he described how the phenomena that we see, including ourselves, are like shadows on the back wall of a cave. We look only at the wall, not the space around and behind us. So we do not see the light source at the cave entrance, and we do not see the "real" forms around us that throw the shadows.

Plato let one "more advanced" cave dweller turn around and walk to the outside world. When he came back and told his companions that they were seeing only illusions of real things, and that an unbelievably bright light source illuminates the world, they did not believe and ridiculed him.

Other prominent philosophers voiced similar opinions. Immanuel Kant (1724 – 1804) said that we do not see the actual "thing-in-itself," and that our three-dimensional space and time do not represent true reality, but that they are illusions of the human mind. Albert Einstein came to a similar conclusion.

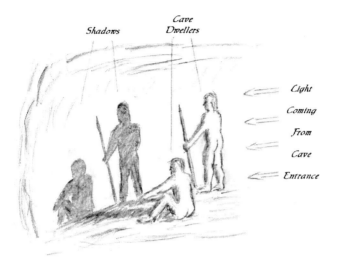

Figure 1.1.   Plato's cave dwellers

We may understand this notion better through an analogy. News media present the daily stock market changes as graphs, showing with a jagged line how the Dow Jones, the NASDAQ, and other market indices change with time. We know that the graph is not the actual thing described. It is only a grossly simplified presentation of what actually occurs. In reality, many thousands, perhaps millions of people try to forecast the potential gains or losses of their investments and decide to buy or sell. They place their orders with a broker, and he arranges the transactions. Countless such trades occur between sellers and buyers in a day. A whole financial culture is active behind the scenes. To obtain an overview of this complex activity, the prices of a number of representative companies are tallied and summarized to create what is called an index. Its value is plotted as a simple, one-line graph versus the time of day, and this is what we see. It would be impossible for you to witness all the individual activities and obtain a meaningful picture of what is going on. The graph does this for you. You accept the graph as a symbol of reality.

Similarly, our 3-D space and time and our entire physical world, is made up of patterns that symbolize what actually occurs behind the scenes. We would not be able to cope with the vastness of what actually occurs. Humans have become so accustomed to these symbols that they see them as reality, forgetting the true reality behind the symbols. We understand that the Dow Jones graph is just a simplified version of business reality. We do not make this connection in our physical world.

Scientists are aware of the fact that our perception does not portray reality. Perhaps the most dramatic discovery of this kind is Albert Einstein's Theory of Relativity that we'll discuss later. One of its conclusions is that our concepts of space and time do not agree with true reality. Instead, we live in an environment in which space and time do not exist as different aspects of reality. We find it difficult to accept that space and time do not exist because everyone thinks that they do. But consider how a person under hypnosis easily accepts deceptive suggestions from a hypnotist. According to Jane Roberts and many other authors writing about spiritual matters, all of humankind is in just such a state of self-administered hypnosis and it is "time" to let go of this misconception. Now, almost 2 ½ millennia after Plato, it has become critical for us to grasp the full meaning of his allegory. As long as we keep an erroneous picture of reality, we will make erroneous decisions that will get us into trouble.

In the early 20th century, Edwin Abbott Abbott (that's his name, 2xAbbott) published a little book titled *Flatland*. He can help us to understand what Plato and

Kant meant.   Abbott described, in humorous detail, creatures that live in a flat, two-dimensional (2-D) space. The space in which they live has no third dimension. Their world is confined to a flat surface, like a sheet of paper with no thickness.

For our discussion, we will modify Abbott's story somewhat. We'll assume that these creatures are circular discs with zero thickness, and that they have a nose, so that we'll know which way they're facing (Fig.1.2). Let's call them "2Ds." Since they are totally flat and can sense only 2-D objects, our 2Ds do not know that a third dimension exists. They can't even imagine 3-D space because nothing in their world gives them a clue that it exists. Any 2D oddball who would suggest that true reality has three dimensions would be ridiculed because everyone knows, of course, that 2-D space is the only reality there is.

If any of us would touch their flat world with one finger, the 2Ds would interpret this as a fellow 2D occupant of their world. If they see it for the first time, they would think that they have discovered a new species. They might call it UFO (for Unknown Foreign Object). The 2Ds do not see the fingerprint pattern because to them it resembles the inner organs of the UFO. If we touch the 2-D world with five fingers of one hand, the 2Ds would see five separate and different UFOs.

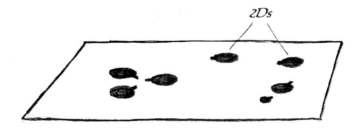

Figure 1.2. 2-D world.

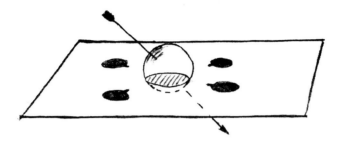

Figure 1.3. Sphere penetrating 2-D world.

Now let's penetrate the plane with a billiard ball, moving it through the plane until it comes out on the other side. The 2Ds would see a circular phenomenon appear. It will grow to a certain size and then shrink again until it disappears completely (Fig.1.3). Some 2D philosophers will believe that this phenomenon didn't really die, but that it continues to exist in some mysterious realm that they call 'spiritual,' even though they have no visible evidence of this in their 2-D world. But most 2Ds will follow the prevailing paradigm of scientific materialism and ignore such "unscientific" notions.

Finally, we'll cut a nail into small pieces so that we have a number of small cylinders and we'll throw them onto the 2-D plane (Fig.1.4). Some cylinders land on their ends, others on their sides. This event creates great excitement among the 2D scientists. They investigate this matter and observe that two different kinds of bodies have appeared in their world, circles and rods. We know, of course, that the cylinder ends show up in their plane as circles, and the cylinder sides as rods. They are just two different aspects of one thing.

Then the 2D scientists discover that they can convert circles into rods and vice versa by causing them to collide with each other. From our 3-D world, we'll see that some cylinders are tipped over on their sides and vice versa. The 2D scientists agonize about this puzzle for decades. Finally, they are forced to assume that the circles and rods are really the same thing that exists in some 'nonmaterial' form. Their wholes do not exist in the 2-D space. The 2Ds postulate that a transcendent 3-D reality exists beyond their world. The term transcendent is defined as 'beyond the limits of normal experience,' or 'beyond the present environment.'

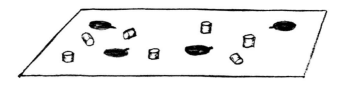

Figure 1.4. 3-D cylinders seen from the 2-D world.

This is how our scientists were puzzled about the nature of light for some 200 years. Around 1700, Isaac Newton postulated that light consists of tiny particles that travel though space like microscopic buckshot. Approximately a hundred years later, scientists concluded that this was an incorrect assumption. Instead, they had proven that light was a form of electro-magnetic radiation, like our radio waves now, but with a much shorter wavelength.

Yet one hundred years later physicists were forced to change their minds again. They had discovered that light can knock electrons around as if miniscule billiard balls were colliding with each other. Based on Albert Einstein's analysis, the scientific community finally accepted that light is both particle and wave. The light particles/waves are now called "photons." We cannot picture them. For us it's like imagining a hole that is round and square at the same time.

Our analogy of the 2D creatures, that see either rods or circles but not the whole object, helps us to understand this concept. The 2Ds can only visualize flat 2-D objects. The rods and circles they see are flat. If a three-dimensional object intersects with their flat world, they see only that portion of the object that coincides with their plane, the rest is invisible to them and therefore unimaginable. They can't imagine a 3-D piece of nail.

Now, moving up one dimension, we know that we experience our world as three-dimensional. Objects have width, depth and height. If there is such a thing as a four-dimensional object, we can't see it and can't imagine it. All we would see of a 4-D object is that part of it that intersects with our 3-D space. In the case of a photon, this part happens to be either a particle or a wave. Both of these are familiar 3-D phenomena for us. We see them separately but not as one object.

The reality is that the photon has more than three dimensions. Two different aspects of it show up in our 3-D world. The photon exists in a world that is *transcendent* to ours; it is beyond our normal experience. It transcends our experience simply by exceeding our limits of perception. This does not mean that the photon does not exist in our 3-D world. It does mean that it exists **not only** here, but also beyond. If we push a pencil through a sheet of paper, does the pencil exist in the paper? Yes it does, but only a small fraction of it. The rest of the pencil is *transcendent* to the paper.

Try not to be turned off by this seemingly mysterious concept. It takes some getting used to. The key issue here is that we humans experience only a small fraction of reality. We must learn to think outside the box. The box, in this case, is our belief that we live in a three-dimensional environment, which is not true. In reality, we live in a world of many more dimensions, but we sense only three of them.

This book is about expanding your consciousness beyond your self-imposed limitations. Warm up to the idea that an everyday experience such as seeing light, is actually an encounter with a phenomenon that transcends your present concepts.

The important point here is that the true reality in which we live has many more dimensions than the three of our physical world. We are indeed like the 2D creatures, unaware of the true reality around us. The concept of multi-dimensional reality may initially feel a little esoteric. This is only because we try to understand it with our limited three-dimensional view. The human mind is perfectly capable of dealing with true reality, but to perceive it, we have to let go of our misconceptions. There is no need to force everything into a three-dimensional box.

For instance, we are quite comfortable with thoughts, even though they encompass literally infinite dimensions. Our thoughts can take us easily into countless different directions beyond the physical three. Think of ideas such as honor, love, hate, and success. They have nothing to do with three-dimensional space. Yet they exist – not physically – but they are real in their own way. They are so real that people have died for them. Thoughts exist in dimensions that are different from those of our physical reality.

This mysterious dual wave/particle nature does not apply only to photons. Physicists found that it applies to all basic material elements. We are familiar with the model of an atom with a nucleus in the center and electrons orbiting around it. We know electrons are minute particles. They flow through wires as electrical current, they hit our TV screens to form pictures, and they run our computers. They are also waves. Scientists use this wave characteristic in the electron microscope. The electron microscope has a much higher resolution than an optical microscope because the electrons' wavelength is much shorter than that of light. Instead of glass lenses, the electron microscope uses magnetic fields that bend the trajectories of the electrically charged electrons.

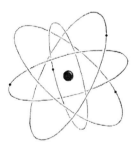

Just like the photon, the electron shows up either as a particle or as a wave, but the "real" electron transcends them both. It has both aspects simultaneously but we can perceive them only one at a time. In other words, the electron has more dimensions than our perception (width, depth and height). Physicists have determined that even the much heavier nucleus of an atom is composed of parts with the wave/particle duality. So all material objects consist of such mysterious entities that are transcendent to our 3-D space.

Imagine what this means. Each item we see and touch is actually a derivative of something that exists in a world with more dimensions than our world – dimensions that are beyond our perception. We are indeed like the 2D creatures that see rods and circles, thinking that they are the real thing, while they are only footprints of the objects that are "really real." Just as Plato said 2,400 years ago, we are like cave dwellers who mistake shadows for reality.

Let's consider this idea more closely, because it is fundamental to the theme of this book and you should become comfortable with it. We tend to resist accepting facts that change our view of the world. We feel uncomfortable giving up the old ideas that have worked for us so far. It takes effort to change, so why bother? We better bother because, simply put, our old ideas no longer work. They were sufficient for the development of sophisticated science and technology, but has humanity really advanced? We are still killing each other and managing to make life miserable for ourselves and our environment. It is our lack of understanding of the dimensions beyond our three-dimensional physical reality that causes our problems.

We are now expanding our vision to encompass new domains that only appear mysterious because we are not used to them. I remember a hilarious movie of the 80's, titled *The Gods Must be Crazy* that took place in Africa. Someone dropped an empty coke bottle from an airplane over the Kalahari Desert. A Bushman found it and was amazed about this strange, beautiful object that had come from the heavens. He showed it to his family where it created quite a stir. Eventually, its many wonderful features and uses led to disputes and violence between family members and the head of the family decided to travel to the end of the world to return the bottle to the Gods. The Bushman's family could not cope with the unknown.

In another analogy, no one would have believed 200 years ago that we would be able to see live pictures from around the world in our living rooms. Radio waves had not yet been discovered and the concept of electromagnetic radiation over long distances was foreign to popular thinking. It was part of an unknown reality. Similarly, we are now becoming aware of the fact that we live in a multi-dimensional reality of which we see only three.

Let's talk a little more about the concept of dimensions. Our common understanding of three-dimensional space is clear. We can also easily picture lower-dimensional spaces. A two-dimensional area is a plane that has width and depth, but no height. A one-dimensional extension is a line, where we can proceed only forward and backward, but not sideways or up and down. The line, incidentally, may be curved and crooked but as long as we can only move lengthwise along the line, it is considered one-dimensional. Time is an example of a one-dimensional environment. We think we can only proceed in one direction in time. Going to a still lower dimension, a point with no extension in any direction is zero-dimensional. Scientists often call dimensions "degrees of freedom." This term expresses the meaning more clearly. If you have the freedom to proceed in only two independent directions, you are in a two-dimensional reality.

In addition to space and time, scientists and engineers refer to dimensions for other parameters such as weight, temperature, and voltage. Modern science routinely deals with more dimensions than three. Scientists talk about five, ten or n-dimensional spaces. Since it is mathematically possible to define such higher-dimensional spaces, experts feel comfortable in using them, even if no one can visualize these spaces. In quantum mechanics (the theory of atoms and subatomic particles) scientists routinely work with hundreds of dimensions to predict atomic behavior with excellent results. Physicists consider these higher-dimensional spaces abstract tools.

Beyond those strictly scientific meanings, we also talk about dimensions when we want to express something that extends beyond a given area of interest. The entire realm of human mental and spiritual activity represents dimensions that do not fit into the "degrees of freedom" considered by the natural sciences. Yet, feelings such as love, pain, or loyalty have a reality of their own. They exist in dimensions that are beyond the range of contemporary science.

Additionally, we use the term dimension whenever we refer to something that exceeds given limitations. Education opens up new dimensions for development. Ludwig van Beethoven ushered in a new dimension in musical history. Space travel is a new dimension in human endeavor, and the September 11 terrorist attack opened an entirely new dimension in warfare. Humanity is now becoming aware of new dimensions that can be pursued for magnificent growth. Let's make sure that we don't ignore them.

INVISIBLE REALITY RESEARCH

If there is a reality that extends beyond ours, it's important that we become acquainted with it. Columbus did this after becoming aware that the Earth is a sphere. How this bit of knowledge expanded our horizon! Columbus' venture is a good analogy of our present situation. For the Europeans of his time, America was invisible and unknown, yet it was real. The scientific discovery of a new dimension prompted its

exploration. The new dimension was the Earth's three-dimensional nature rather than that of a two-dimensional plane, as people had believed. We are now in a similar situation. The real world has more dimensions than the three of which we are aware, and we can explore new worlds by venturing beyond our three-dimensional limitation. We can turn around like Plato's cave dweller who discovered the true reality.

Religions have always fostered a belief in an invisible reality. According to most religious doctrines, individuals continue to live after death in a nonphysical environment. Many scientists do not agree with this. They believe that physical matter is the fundamental substance from which everything else has evolved. Even life itself is believed to have come from chance interactions of material parts, such as atoms and molecules. The spectacular success of our technology which has resulted from scientific research supports the scientists' confidence in these beliefs. However, physics is the science of physical reality. Its very charter makes it biased. If you ask a carpenter to build a house, he will build one of wood. If you ask a mason to build a house, it will be of bricks, and if you ask a physicist to create a model of the universe, it will be a physical one.

Yet, for almost a century, physical science has not been able to make a major breakthrough in understanding the basic nature of reality comparable to the discovery of quantum physics. This is not due to a lack of excellent scientists; the best minds in the world have tackled it. This kind of evolutionary slowdown is typical before a major thrust into a different direction. This book, along with others, outlines this new direction.

One physicist who bucked the prevailing scientific view was David Bohm (1917 – 1992). Born in Pennsylvania, he eventually served as Professor of Theoretical Physics at the University of London. He was Einstein's protégé and is known as an outstanding quantum physicist of his time. Throughout his career, Bohm tried to understand the nature of ultimate reality behind the phenomena of our world. He believed that the process of how we describe physical phenomena with our limited language prejudices our view of reality. Based on his intimate understanding of quantum theory and relativity theory, Bohm concluded that the seemingly separate physical phenomena are actually projections from an undivided, constantly changing, universal whole that he called *holomovement*. David Bohm believed that the holomovement consisted of an invisible *implicate order* and a visible *explicate order*, where the explicate emerged from the implicate order. In Bohm's opinion, life and consciousness were part of the implicate order, and they dwelled within all visible objects, including what we call inanimate matter. Most physicists rejected David Bohm's concepts during his time.

Today a growing number of physicists are trying to find the unity of science and spirituality. Fritjof Capra wrote his best-selling book *The Tao of Physics,* in which he explored the parallels between quantum physics and the Eastern religious philosophies of Hinduism, Buddhism, and Taoism. He stated, "modern physics leads us to a view of the world which is very similar to the views held by mystics of all ages and traditions."

In 1993, Amit Goswami, together with R.E. Reed and M. Goswami, published a book titled *The Self-Aware Universe – how consciousness creates the material world.* While writing this book, Goswami gained the insight that consciousness is not a product of the brain, as contemporary science still believes. Instead, consciousness is the ground of all being. As his friend Joel said in a pivotal discussion, "Consciousness is prior and unconditional. It is all there is. There is nothing but God." After this realization, Amit Goswami discovered that all the seeming paradoxes of quantum physics could be explained. Amit Goswami, PhD, is professor of physics at the Institute of Theoretical Sciences at the University of Oregon. Other physicists who published books about how modern science leads to spirituality include Fritjof Capra, Paul Davies, Norman Friedmann, and Fred Alan Wolf,.

One aspect of invisible reality is the question of life after death. The mainstream scientific community completely avoids addressing this issue. We would assume that modern science, with all its advanced methods, should be able to come up with a definite answer to this vital question. Imagine how a clear answer would benefit the world! We are not asking them to prove or disprove a religious belief. We want to understand Reality, with a capital R, regardless of religious and scientific prejudices.

One expert who investigated the afterlife question is Dr. Ian Stevenson, Professor of Psychiatry at the University of Virginia Medical School. Over several decades he has made a landmark contribution by performing thousands of scientifically documented case studies of what appears to be reincarnation. Based on his impeccable professional credibility, the Virginia University Press decided to publish volumes of case histories researched by Dr. Stevenson and his team (*Reincarnation and Biology* 1997, others). Sylvia Cranston and Carey Williams summarized Dr. Stevenson's work in a 1984 book titled, *Reincarnation.*

Dr. Stevenson focused his attention on children, because he observed that reincarnational memory fades after a certain age, and that the spontaneous recollection of children is less likely to be biased. Dr. Stevenson also explains that children's stories could be verified because witnesses to their former lives could still be alive. According to the reports, he and his staff taped interviews with about twenty-five witnesses for each case investigated. They checked out documents, letters, medical records, etc., and compared character traits between the interviewed child and what they believed was the child's former personality. It is written that in hundreds of cases, the child could point to a birthmark where it claimed to have been wounded or killed in its former life, and the correlation of the wound could be verified through witnesses or records of these events. In one of the examples, a boy claimed that he was formerly a Turkish bandit who took his life when he was cornered by authorities. He shot himself from below through his jaw.

The boy had a large mark there, and hair was missing on his scalp where the bullet supposedly had emerged in his former life. A witness to the shooting was still alive and verified these details, according to the account. Other reported cases involved people who could speak foreign languages fluently, although they had never learned them in their present lives. Many such examples are provided, and the evidence that reincarnation exists appears convincing.

Another expert on the afterlife question is Dr. Victor Zammit. His Internet website, *A Lawyer Presents The Case For The Afterlife* (http://www.ozemail.com) informs us that for many years he has researched an overwhelming amount of evidence about psychic phenomena recorded on millions of pages and supported by scientific research. Dr. Zammit is convinced that, when taken as a whole, the evidence absolutely and unqualifiedly proves that life after death exists. Using his professional background as an attorney and his university training in psychology, history and science, Dr. Zammit states that the many credible examples would constitute objective evidence in the Supreme Court of the United States, the House of Lords in England, the High Court of Australia and in every civilized legal jurisdiction around the world.

Chapter 2

The Whole And Its Parts

We have discussed that our view of the world does not present true reality. We see only a fraction of what is, and even that appears distorted. Our consciousness lacks the scope to grasp all existing dimensions. The analogy of the 2D-creatures demonstrated how this can occur. It is better for us to understand this, because if we don't, then we will make mistakes. It's like traveling without a roadmap. Humanity has come to a fork in the road of evolution, and it's vital for us to find out which way to go. Fortunately, we can make enough observations in our environment to construct our own roadmap of reality. We can do this as follows:

We'll observe that everything in the universe is organized into wholes and parts. This is so evident that we take it for granted. From galaxies down to subatomic particles, from an entire ecosystem to a cell's chromosomes, from libraries to the letters of the alphabet, every whole consists of component parts, which in turn have even smaller parts.

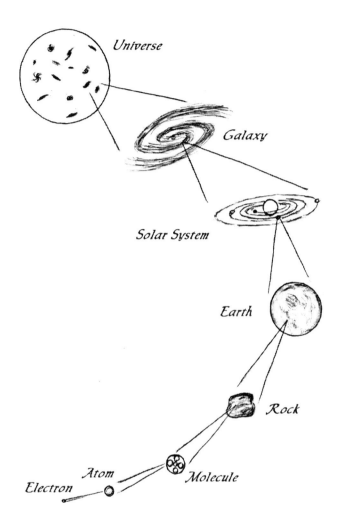

Figure 1.5. Wholes and parts in the universe

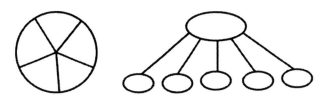

Figure 1.6. Two diagrams of wholes and their parts

Wholes and Parts, or in philosophical terms, universals and particulars, are everywhere. Yet their relationship to each other is not understood. We say that the whole is more than the sum of its parts, but we are not clear as to how this is. For instance, we think of a person having a body and a mind, but to this day, science does not understand how they function together to form a whole being. Let's take an ant colony, for instance. The whole community functions as a well-organized unit, acting like one individual entity, while the ants pursue their own individual tasks in perfect union with the interests of the whole.

The Hungarian philosopher and author Arthur Koestler introduced the term "holon" for an individual entity that is a part of a greater whole, and that itself is made up of component parts, as indicated in Figure 1.5. The parts are entities in their own right, with sub-parts of their own. Throughout history, philosophers have debated the relationship between wholes and their parts. For instance, how can something be whole and yet divided? Or: which of the two is real, the universal or its particulars? We do not want to get bogged down in debates upon which even historical luminaries such as Plato and Aristotle could not agree. Nevertheless, it may surprise you that we can build a reality map of the whole universe, visible and invisible, by paying attention to the inner relationships of wholes and parts.

This is an abstract issue, but it is fundamental to understanding our world. With this understanding we can do a better job of living in it. To bring the abstract "down to earth," we will use analogies and practical examples. Imagine a cut crystal, like a diamond. Consider its form, ignoring its material substance (Fig.1.7). The form represents a three-dimensional whole unit, and the two-dimensional planes of the crystal sides are the parts that make up the whole. Each part represents an aspect of the whole.

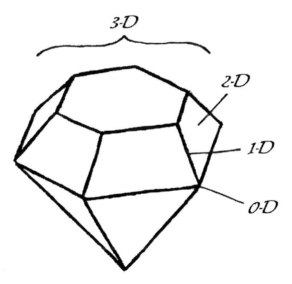

Figure 1.7.   Crystal form.

Using this model, we can make important observations concerning the relationship between wholes and their parts. I call these relationships "Holon Principles," each with a designator, **HP1**, **HP2**, **HP3**, etc. for easy reference. And I call the combined whole of these Holon Principles "Holistic Logic."

Let's start with the first observation, the first Holon Principle. The whole crystal form has three dimensions, but its parts, the surface planes, have only two dimensions each. The whole exists on a "higher dimensional level" than its parts. It would help you to develop a feeling for this relationship. Imagine being a 2D creature in one of the planes. From this viewpoint, the whole crystal is "transcendent," because it is beyond the dimensions of the planes.

We'll continue to adopt different viewpoints throughout this discussion, switching between different dimensions, because we want to obtain an intuitive feeling for these relationships, rather than simply an abstract knowledge. This brings you closer to experiencing the true nature of our reality. It can even bring you closer to experiencing the true nature of yourself. Ultimately, this is what life is all about, an experience from different levels of consciousness. For now we experience it from the level of the parts. Eventually we want to open up our consciousness to experience the whole reality.

We state now the first Holon Principle:

HP1.* The number of dimensions of the whole exceeds that of its individual parts.

Examples will help you to become more familiar with how wholes have more dimensions than their parts. Take your time and try to visualize how this Holon Principle applies.

Rainbow Colors

Consider the colors of a rainbow. When we send a narrow white light beam through a prism, it fans out on the other side into different colors of light, ranging from red through violet (Fig.1.8a). Similarly, individual raindrops split white sunlight into different colors. If we reverse the prism experiment, sending the colored beams back through the prism in the opposite direction, we obtain pure white light again (Fig.1.8b). This means that white light is not colorless, but that it is the whole of all colors combined. Therefore, white light with its parts, the colors, are a **holon.** (As mentioned before, a holon is an individual entity that is a part of a greater whole and that itself is made up of component parts. White light is part of the entire electro-magnetic frequency spectrum and itself is made up of component parts, the colors.)

---

* The Holon Principles in this book are refined over those listed in my 1991 essay *Revolution in Common Sense*, website http://home.sprynet.com/~jowolf

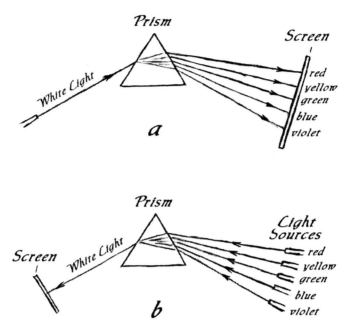

Figure 1.8a. White light separates into rainbow colors

Figure 1.8b. Rainbow colors combine to make white
light

Let's test **HP1** for this example. Light waves vibrate
with a certain frequency, about a million billion cycles per
second. Each color of light has a different frequency and
the white light covers the whole frequency range of
colors. Since white light extends over a range of different
frequencies while each color is only a single frequency,
white light has one more dimension than each of its
individual colors. It is like a 1-D line versus a 0-D point.
This satisfies Holon Principle **HP1**. The number of
dimensions of the whole exceeds those of its individual
parts.

Television

We are all familiar with holons in the field of information, such as television or newspapers. A TV camera scans the image to be transmitted similar to the way we read text, one horizontal line at a time, from the top of the page to its bottom, and then back to the top of the next page. In TV, the equivalent of a page is called a "frame" (Fig.1.9). Hundreds of lines cover a frame so

Figure 1.9. TV frame

that the eye hardly perceives them. To create the impression of a continuous picture, the camera repeats frames so fast that the eye can't separate them (50 or 60 per second). This process is similar to that of a movie. Each frame is a still picture, a "snapshot," and the fast succession of individual still pictures creates the impression of a moving scene. The camera senses color and the intensity of each individual dot along each line within a frame. This information is converted into a running electrical signal that is broadcast (Fig.1.10). TV receivers convert it back to the original picture in a reverse process.

Figure 1.10. TV signal

Let's call a moving TV scene the "whole" to be transmitted.   Its "parts" are the individual frames sent many times a second.   They are a series of snapshots like the frames in a movie.

According to **HP1**, the whole has more dimensions than each of its parts, thus the scene has more dimensions than each individual picture, because the scene shows motion and the individual picture doesn't.

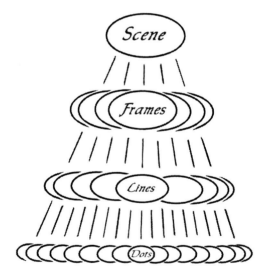

Figure 1.11, TV transmission holarchy
(hierarchy of holons)

Note that we have a multilevel hierarchy in the TV example (Fig.1.11). Koestler called a hierarchy of holons a "holarchy." While an individual TV frame is a part of the transmitted scene, it is also a whole for the individual scanned lines that are the parts. The whole frame has two dimensions (vertical and horizontal), one more than its parts, the 1-D horizontal lines that have only one dimension. Here too the whole has more dimensions than each of its parts. One dimensional level down, the individual lines, while being parts of a frame, are also wholes for all the dots along the line. The line has one dimension. Its dots have zero.

The Human Body

In a complex system such as the human body (Fig.1.12), we can't use the limited concept of three-dimensional space. Three dimensions cannot describe the intricate functions involved. Rather we can use the term 'dimension' in the broader sense mentioned at the end of Chapter 1, indicating a range of potential or capability.

Each part of the body has its own specialty. The muscles flex, the skin protects, the eyes see, the heart pumps blood, etc. Each part performs a specific "dimension" of the overall body's function. The whole of the body performs all of them in a coordinated manner. Therefore, the whole has more dimensions than each of its parts.

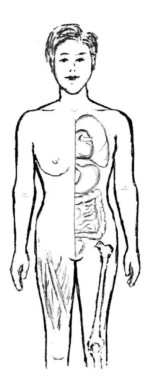

Figure 1.12. Human body

The Self

We each have a mind and a body but the Self transcends them both.   The Self must have more dimensions than either body or mind because it includes them both and coordinates them into a living entity. We'll use the word "Self" capitalized when we mean the inner, higher Self of a person.

The Photon

We have already encountered Holon Principle One when we talked about a subatomic unit such as a photon or an electron. These units have the mysterious dual quality of appearing in our physical world either as a wave or as a particle. However, once we recognize that these appearances are actually different aspects of the same whole, then the mystery becomes quite plausible. Subatomic units, such as the photon, have more than three dimensions. Their wholes are transcendent to our 3-D view. Being transcendent does not mean that they aren't real. It only means that there's room for our perception to grow. The purpose of this book is to expand our perception to include the larger reality in which we live.

Chapter 3

More Holon Principles

The Holon Principles describe the relationship between a whole and its parts. We discussed the first and perhaps most important Holon Principle in the preceding chapter, along with several examples to deepen your understanding of this relationship. Chapter 3 explains the remaining nine Holon Principles, using the crystal model and the previous examples.

Developing an intuitive knowledge of the relationships between wholes and their parts is important when we investigate higher dimensions. It is not as important that you intellectually understand them as it is that you open your mind and understand with your heart. The Holon Principles are but steps towards an intuitive knowledge of holistic reality. This leads you to insights beyond your present understanding, and it enables you to address important issues in your life that now seem beyond your reach.

In the crystal model, we observe that the 3-D crystal unites all its 2-D side planes into one entity. We can express this as the second Holon Principle. Notice that we are making this observation with our customary three-dimensional view, which matches the dimensions of the whole crystal.

HP2. **The whole and its parts are one, when viewed from the dimensional level of the whole.**

We have already seen in our rainbow color example that the whole of white light unites all colors into one single entity.

On the TV screen, the whole scene unites its sequential frames into one cohesive entity. Also, in the TV transmission holarchy of Figure 1.11, each frame is a whole that unites its scanned lines into a single undivided entity. And at the next lower dimensional level, each line is a whole that unites its dots into one entity.

The human body's parts are united into a single, undivided entity, when seen from the whole's viewpoint. You also know that your mind and body are united into the one entity you call your Self.

And scientific research has determined that the photon and its parts, particle and wave, represent one unit. The same holds true for the electron and all other subatomic units, even though we can't see these relationships directly because our daytime consciousness is not on the multi-dimensional level of the subatomic units. This leads us to the next Holon Principle.

Now we are shifting our consciousness away from the whole and are assuming the role of one of the parts. Remember that the 2D creatures in figure 1.2 perceived only their 2-D world. They didn't see anything that was not in their plane of existence. If they were to live in one of the crystal planes, they would not see the whole crystal. It exists in the higher third dimension that transcends their world. This leads us to the third Holon Principle.

HP3.   The whole is invisible from the lower dimensional level of its parts.

Notice how our state of mind can change the reality we see. An impressionist painter viewing a forest at a distance will see it as one single whole, but a "realist" will paint the individual trees. A perfectionist may not even see the forest for its trees. Or a general viewing a parade may see a column of soldiers as one single unit, but the young girl looking for her sweetheart sees the individual soldiers.

Figure 1.13, Impressionist versus realistic painting

Our viewpoint makes the difference. The reality is the same, but we choose to see it differently. We use these different viewpoints many times every day when experiencing different circumstances. However, as soon as we encounter a situation that transcends our familiar dimensions, we are confounded. For example when a loved one dies, our eyes can see only his three-dimensional body; they cannot see his immortal multi-dimensional whole.

To see how **HP3** works in the rainbow example, let's assume a part's viewpoint and identify with a single color, say red, by looking through a red color filter at the white light, which is the whole of all colors. We can see only red and not white, meaning that we do not see the whole from the part's viewpoint. This is what **HP3** states.

In our television example, we can't see the whole show by looking at one individual frame that contains only a still picture. Or, going one level lower in the TV holarchy, we can't see the whole picture contained in one frame when only one of its scan-lines is exposed on the screen. Moving down one more step, we don't see the whole line if we focus only at one dot through a magnifying glass.

The next example we used earlier is the human body. We don't see it when we look at only one of its parts. Similarly, your eyes cannot see your whole Self, and neither can your conscious mind. You sense that your Self is there, but your mind does not perceive it objectively. The reason is that your whole Self has more dimensions than your waking consciousness. You are even less able to perceive the Selves in others. They dwell in multi-dimensional reality, as your own Self does, invisible from the lower dimensional levels of your eyes and your conscious mind.

We now understand why scientists can't observe the photon or electron itself, while seeing its two aspect parts, particle and wave. Our three-dimensional mindsets and our laboratory equipment simply can't perceive the multi-dimensional domain that has four and more dimensions. Plato already told us that we don't perceive true reality, as did Immanuel Kant and others. We use our concepts of 3-D space and time like a blind man uses his hands to sense what he cannot see. Our concepts of space and time are inadequate dimensions to present the true reality.

In the crystal analogy, we can imagine that all surface planes are populated with 2D creatures. However, for the 2D creatures in any one particular plane, the others are outside their 2-D world, transcendent in 3-D space, and therefore invisible. Thus we can assume that other 3-D worlds exist elsewhere in the invisible multi-dimensional reality, and they may well be populated too. Our astronauts may find no life on Mars, while whole cities could thrive there in dimensions that Earthlings do not see. This is not an idle thought. Quantum physicists are seriously considering the existence of invisible realities that are "parallel" to ours. We will explore this subject later.

Figure 1.14. Astronaut on Mars with "ghost" city
in other dimensions.

This is quite an exciting thought! The Holon Principles convey new concepts. They may appear difficult because you are not accustomed to consciously switching back and forth between different points of view. I promise that you will be well rewarded for your effort when you follow this train of thought. Your mind will be able to sense the grandeur of your own soul and the magnificence of the universe.

Let's continue with another analogy. Suppose you inspect a house that is up for sale. You walk around it and take a picture of each side to show your husband (Fig. 1.15). When he comes home from work, he sees the pictures and thinks that they are of four different houses. You have to explain that they are photos of the same house. Your husband did not see this because the pictures are quite different and because they are only two-dimensional. Had you shown him a three-dimensional model of the house, he would have seen immediately the shape of the whole house. His problem was that he saw the different aspects of the house as separate two-dimensional entities. The third dimension that ties the four 2-D aspects together into a whole was missing.

Front   *Right Side*   *Rear*   *Left Side*

Figure 1.15.   Four aspects of a house.

In our crystal analogy (Fig. 1.7), each plane of the crystal is only one of the crystal's aspects. A 2D creature living in one of the planes would not know this, because it can't imagine a three-dimensional object with many aspects. It would experience its home plane as the only one there is. This plane would be separated from the other planes, because our 2D creature is unable to go around a corner into 3-D space. Yet all planes are parts of one crystal. Thus the parts seem separated in their own 2D world while they are actually just different aspects of one 3D whole. Therefore we can formulate the fourth Holon Principle:

HP4. **The different aspects of the whole appear as separated parts, when viewed from the lower dimensional level of the parts.**

HP4 must be understood together with **HP3.** The whole is invisible, *and* its different aspects appear as separated parts when viewed from the lower dimensional level of the parts. We can visualize the fourth Holon Principle by using the examples cited under **HP1.** In the rainbow example we saw the different colors that are the parts of white light. The colors are aspects of white light. After sending white light through a prism, we see the colors as separated parts, corresponding to **HP4**, because we see them now at the lower dimensional level of single frequencies. Remember, the whole of white light covers a range of color frequencies, which represents a higher dimension than a single color frequency. This is similar to how a line represents a higher dimension than a dot.

In the television example, a scene on the TV screen is composed of individual frames that change fifty or sixty times per second. These "snapshot" frames represent aspects of the whole scene. Corresponding to **HP4,** the frames appear as separate parts of the scene when we look at them as individual still pictures. They are at the lower dimensional level of the parts compared with the moving scene.

Going down the TV transmission holarchy of figure 1.11, the scanned lines are aspects of each frame. To see this, please focus your consciousness on the one-dimensional world of lines. They appear as separate parts when we look at them from this perspective. Moving one step lower yet, the individual dots along each line are aspects of each line and are separate parts at their own 0-D level.

In the human body, the different functional aspects of the whole are represented by separate organs when viewed from the lower dimensional level of the parts. Our bodies and minds are aspects of our whole Selves when viewed from the viewpoint of the mind. And the two different aspects of photons appear as separate parts (particles and waves) when seen from our lower three-dimensional level.

Some of the above statements may seem self-evident. As indicated before, the purpose of stating them here is to expose you to the process of looking at a situation from different perspectives, of changing your viewpoint and the focus of your consciousness. We'll keep switching our points of view between the whole and its parts. This is like moving our attention from a forest to its trees and back to the forest again.

It is very important to become conscious of the change in our points of view. In everyday matters, we often change viewpoints automatically without noticing. However, when we encounter holons that exist in multi-dimensional reality, such as the photons and electrons mentioned earlier, or psychological and spiritual issues, then we can easily be confused by not being aware of the point of view. In fact, being unaware of differences in viewpoints causes most of the world's problems.

Some scientists are of the opinion that the multi-dimensional whole of the photon is not real, because it does not exist in the 3-D world that we perceive. Many people would claim that something is real only if it can be physically sensed. However, using Holistic Logic, we know that dimensions beyond ours exist, and that our consciousness determines what is real for us and what is not. This book is about consciousness.

HP2 taught us that the whole and its individual parts are one. Therefore, if anything is real within a holon, then everything else in it must also be real. Simple enough. However, we also say that the whole is more than the sum of its parts. This is true because the whole is united into a coordinated system, whereas the sum of the parts is not. We know that a united whole is more powerful than its separate parts. Just think of a well-coordinated sports team versus a collection of players meeting for the first time. Therefore we are justified in stating the following Holon Principle:

HP5.   The reality of the whole is more significant than that of its parts.

We could have just restated the well-known expression, "the whole is more than the sum of its parts." However, **HP5** gives a better indication of how the whole is more. It is more in quality rather than quantity. Its quality, power, and intensity of existence are greater than that of its parts. Think of the difference between a human body and its shadow in Plato's cave, or between white light and its colors. The words "the reality is more significant" more accurately characterizes the difference between a whole and its parts.

HP5 is illustrated with the crystal analogy. The whole is the real thing. Its parts are just its aspects. Yet the parts have their individual reality at their own dimensional level. In Plato's cave allegory, the 2-D shadows on the wall do indeed exist – as shadows. They have their own reality, even though they are not "as significantly real" as the actual 3-D objects that create them.

When applying **HP5** to our other holon examples, it makes sense to say that white light has more significant reality than its colors. Also, the live TV scene has a more significant reality than its individual fixed frames. The same is true for the frames as wholes. They are more significant than their scan lines, and the lines themselves are more significant than their dots.

The human body's reality as a whole is more significant than that of its parts because of its greater versatility and its ability compared to the functions of its parts. We think of our whole Selves as more significant than our minds and bodies. We will even go so far as to eventually give up our bodies. And to be consistent, we will assume that the invisible photon is more significantly real in its multi-dimensional reality than as a particle and a wave in our physical world.

The sketch of the universe and its parts, figure 1.5 (Chapter 2) shows how each part of a larger entity is the whole for its component parts. A galaxy is a part of the universe and at the same time it is the whole of many solar systems. A solar system is a part of a galaxy and at the same time it is the whole of its planets, and so on in a hierarchy down to subatomic particles. Figure 1.16, below, demonstrates this holistic characteristic, using the crystal. Each aspect plane is an entity of its own at the 2-D level. We can also go to the next lower level. The lines along the edges of the planes are 1-D parts of the 2-D planes, which are wholes from the line's viewpoint. If we can get our consciousness down to 1-D, or linear, thinking (some people have no difficulty doing this ☺) then we can see that the lines are also entities in their own right within the 1-D order. And finally, the points are aspects of the lines and they can be seen as entities in their 0-D order. Thus we have a hierarchy of holons with four levels of dimensional order (Fig. 1.17).

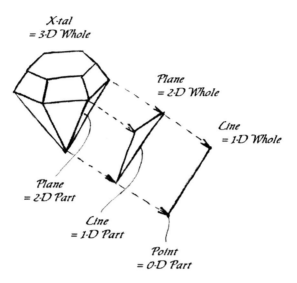

Figure 1.16. Parts are also whole

We can now formulate the sixth Holon Principle:

HP6.   Each part is itself a whole at a lower dimensional level.

In testing **HP6** on our examples, we can say that each colored light is a part of white light, and at the same time it is the whole of its photons. On the top of the light holarchy, white light is the whole of its colors. But it is also a part of a greater whole, all electro-magnetic radiation.

In the TV example, the frames are the parts of a scene, but they are also wholes in their own right, and the scan lines are their parts. The lines are also wholes with the dots as their parts. Finally, the dots are individual wholes, each with its specific color and brightness.

The human body is part of a person, yet it is a whole itself. The body parts are wholes that are composed of cells as their parts, and so on, all the way down to subatomic particles. In our last holon example, scientists regard a photon's parts, the particle and the wave, as whole manifestations, in and of themselves.

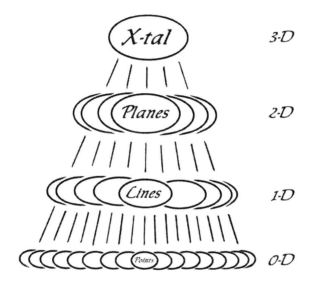

Figure 1.17. Holarchy diagram with four dimensional levels.

To arrive at the next Holon Principle we'll again identify with a part and ask, "where is the whole from this viewpoint?" We can't see it, according to **HP3**. However, because we are one with the whole (**HP2**), we should be able to locate it. For instance, if you identify with mind and are looking from that point of view, then where is your Self? Where is the whole that represents the unity of the mind and the body? When you say, "I feel it in my heart," or, "it is my heart's desire," then you don't really mean the physical heart that pumps the blood, but your essence, your inner Self that is beyond mind and body.

We sense that the whole is inside us. We also know that it transcends the two parts, the mind and the body. The word for something that is inside and simultaneously transcendent is "immanent." Therefore we can say that our wholes are immanent in our minds and our bodies. We can assume that this is true for animals as well. They all appear to be acting from inside out, so their Selves must be immanent.

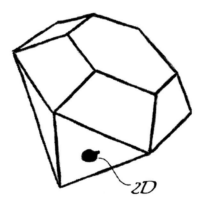

Figure 1.18. For the 2D creature, the crystal is immanent in the 2-D plane.

We can visualize this idea with the crystal analogy. Where is the whole crystal from the viewpoint of the 2D creature shown in figure 1.18? For us it is obvious that the crystal transcends the 2D's plane, that it exists in 3-D space beyond the planar world of the 2D creature. But from the 2D's viewpoint, all we can say is that the crystal is present inside the 2D's plane and transcends it. In other words, it is immanent in its part. Therefore we can state:

HP7.   The whole is immanent in each of its parts.

It is understandable why many believe that our physical world is the true reality.   Since ultimate reality is immanent in each physical object, we can point to the object and claim that it represents ultimate reality. It does indeed.

Let's visit our rainbow color example to test **HP7**. When we think of light, we naturally think of white light. We consider white light the essence of light.   That essence is immanent in any light, regardless of its color. In that sense, white light is immanent in each of its colors.

In the TV example, each frame contains the essence of the whole scene. In other words, each frame provides a good idea of what the program is about. In that sense, the TV scene is immanent in its frames. We are aware of this when we surf through channels to find something interesting.   Moving down one level in the TV transmission holarchy (Fig. 1.11), if we were to see only one scan line of a TV frame, we would notice a color and brightness pattern distributed along its length.   That pattern tells us that the whole frame's image is an arrangement of color and brightness. In that sense, the frame's image pattern is "immanent" in each scan line. How is a whole TV scan line "immanent" in its dot-parts? Each dot has some color and brightness. They represent the essence of a whole scan line: the color and brightness pattern along its length.

In the human body, the body's essence is encoded in its genes and therefore is immanent in all its parts. And finally, the photon is immanent in its particle and wave simply because they represent the photon for us, similar to the way an individual's body represents that person's Self.

The eighth Holon Principle is very important and interesting. Everything in the universe changes continually. This Holon Principle helps us to understand the dynamics involved.

HP8.   A change in a part corresponds to a change in the whole, and a change in the whole corresponds to a change in its parts.

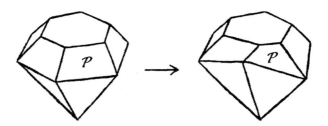

Figure 1.19. The whole and its parts change together.

If we change one part of our crystal, for instance plane P (Fig. 1.19), we change the whole crystal form including other parts. The change of a single part changes the character of the whole. On the other hand, we can also say that a change in the whole corresponds to a change in its parts, by making the same change we just made. We could have decided to give the crystal the form shown on the right. As a result, plane P assumed its new shape. The change is exactly the same in both cases, only our viewpoint is different.

This may seem trivial, like splitting hairs, but when we experience the same situation at a higher dimensional level, we are mystified. Take, for instance, the relationship of mind and body, the parts of the whole Self. A change of mind changes the Self, and this affects the body. Your body is tired when your mind is depressed, or vice versa. The whole enigma of mind-body interaction can be understood holistically. You don't notice a physical change with every single thought, but a major psychological change does affect the body, positively or negatively, depending upon the type of psychological change. Spontaneous healings have been reported after patients were relieved of emotional problems. Excessive mental stress has been known to cause health problems such as stomach ulcers and back pain. We will address this subject in more detail later.

Notice that **HP8** does not say that any part's change **causes** a corresponding change in the whole. The whole changes as the parts change, without one causing the other. This is because the whole and its parts are the same, we are just seeing them from different perspectives. When we changed the P plane in figure 1.19, we felt that this caused the whole crystal to change. But we had this impression only because we assumed the viewpoint of the part. We might also have wanted to change the form of the crystal, and ended up with a new shape for plane P. There is just one reality. Only our viewpoints differ.

So, if a person makes up his mind to change his character, is it his mind that causes the change, or is it the Self, of which the mind is a part? This is a futile question because, in reality, the person is a whole entity. No division exists between the Self and the mind. The whole and its parts are one, when viewed from the dimensional level of the whole (**HP2**). It is the Self's change that is more significant. **HP5** states that the reality of the whole is more significant than that of its parts. We assume separations where none exist because our senses don't have enough dimensions to see the actual multi-dimensional reality.

Let's see how our holon examples demonstrate changes in a holon. Holon Principle 8 contains two statements:

1.)   A change in a part corresponds to a change in the whole.
2.)   A change in the whole corresponds to a change in its parts.

We apply the first of these statements to the rainbow color example and observe that a change of any color means a corresponding change in the whole, which now deviates from pure white light. This occurs as follows.

In the second prism experiment (Fig.1.8b) we reversed the light flow from right to left, so that all color beams flow back into the prism and come out as white light on the left side. If we change any color input on the right, then the combined light on the left will be tinted, depending on what color we changed, and how much. If we increase the red light intensity on the right, then the whole, or combination, of all colors on the left becomes reddish. If we decrease red, the whole becomes more blue.

According to the second statement above, a change in the whole light corresponds to a change in the colors. While conducting the first prism experiment by shining the whole light from the left (Fig. 1.8a), we can change its intensity and all color beams exiting at the right of the prism will change their intensity correspondingly. We can also tint the input light on the left.   Then the composition of the individual colors on the right will also be different.   The only way to tint the whole light is by changing its color content. In other words, the rainbow color test agrees with Holon Principle 8.

In the TV example, when we change the image of any single frame of the whole scene, then we must also change the adjacent frames, or the scene would not be whole any more; the program would be interrupted. Thus any part's change corresponds to a change in the whole. And of course, any change in the whole scene affects its parts, corresponding to **HP8**.   Continuing down the holarchy (Fig. 1.11), we can make the same observations for the frame-wholes and their line-parts, and also for the line-wholes and their dot-parts.

In the human body example, a part's change, such as the loss of a limb, or a heart attack, means a change for the whole body.   Also, any change of the body means that at least one part changes, otherwise there would be no change of the body.

And finally, when a photon's particle and wave move, we associate this with a corresponding change of the multi-dimensional photon itself, and vice versa.

The Holon Principles are not always as clearly recognizable in man-made systems as in our television example.   The reason for this is that we are limited to seeing reality in three dimensions.   When we look at an automobile, for instance, we might think that the first Holon Principle is not valid.   We do not see that the whole car has more dimensions than its parts.   Both the whole car and its parts are three-dimensional.   How does a car illustrate **HP1**?   We need to consider the whole car in the holistic sense, not just look at its three-dimensional structure. When considering the whole car, we should also include everything that makes it a working unit, all the design details, complex interrelationships, mathematical formulas, patents, and whatever else was necessary to evolve the unified functional whole. Only a car designer's mind might perceive this whole picture, and that whole exists in the mental domain, which is multi-dimensional compared with the car's three-dimensional appearance. In this sense, the whole car has more dimensions than its parts.

We were able to formulate Holon Principles one through eight using the three-dimensional crystal example. However Holon Principle eight does not completely describe holistic changes in multi-dimensional reality. Physicists have gained important information about the characteristics of that higher dimensional level. One such characteristic is called 'nonlocality.' This term is used for situations when an action at one location in three-dimensional space triggers a simultaneous action at a distance, even though no connection exists between them in three-dimensional space. Scientists have observed nonlocality in experiments with photons that were created by the same atomic event. After these photons had traveled miles apart through fiber optics, scientists introduced a certain change in one of them. A corresponding change occurred in the other photon instantaneously. This means that a connection existed between both photons that acted faster than light. According to Einstein's well-proven relativity theory, nothing can travel faster than the speed of light. So, how can one photon influence the other after they have traveled apart with the speed of light?

Physicists have advanced different interpretations of this baffling experimental result. The interpretation of nonlocality that is most compatible with Holistic Logic is as follows: Nonlocality means that no localities exist in multi-dimensional reality. In other words, nothing is separated from anything else in terms of spatial location. Space, as we know it, does not exist in multidimensional reality. New York and Paris are not separated in the multi-dimensional environment as they appear to be in our three-dimensional space. They are still different aspects of reality, but not in terms of miles. Remember, different aspects of the whole appear as separate parts, when viewed from the lower dimensional level of the parts (**HP4**). Scientists have tested nonlocality in the world of subatomic particles. Yet, all physical reality is composed of subatomic particles and we may assume that no spatial separation exists in multi-dimensional reality.

We already know that the whole and its parts are one, when viewed from the dimensional level of the whole (**HP2**), and that the different aspects of a whole appear as separate parts, when viewed from the lower dimensional level of the parts. But when we see the crystal as an undivided whole, its planes still appear at different places in space. However, when we move higher to four dimensions, the different aspects of wholes are merged even more, so much so that spatial separation makes no sense. Our concept of space simply does not exist in multi-dimensional reality. What we call space is a human perception, but it is not true reality. The higher proceed up the holarchy, the more everything is unified because we become aware of ever more dimensions as our consciousness expands.

Remember the stock market index metaphor mentioned in Chapter 1. We perceive a simplified symbolic version of true reality. So we see items neatly separated in space, although they are really merged into one incredibly diverse and interwoven whole. Instead of separate items, picture different gases mixed in the same space. Or think of all the electro-magnetic waves permeating our world, from low frequency radio waves and TV signals to microwaves, light, and gamma rays. They all exist together as different aspects of electro-magnetic radiation, yet they are clearly distinguishable. Or think of the contents of your mind. Somehow all your ideas, feelings, memories, and knowledge exist in you. The Stanford neuroscientist Karl Pribram has determined that memories do not reside in different parts of the brain[*], yet you can identify each thought individually. So let us assume that no spatial separation exists between different aspects in multi-dimensional reality. We perceive them as separate in space and time, but in true reality, they are all one giant "ball of wax." I had experienced this characteristic of multi-dimensional reality when I had the vision that I've mentioned in the Introduction. Lack of space separation is an important aspect of Holistic Logic.

HP9.   No divisions and separations exist in multi-dimensional reality.

Now, since the whole is undivided at its level, a change of any part permeates the entire whole. It's like mixing salt into soup. The character of the entire whole changes with the change of any part. And, because the whole is immanent in all its parts, the whole's change in turn affects **all** its parts. The parts are supported now by a changed entity. Their essence, their character has changed. We can formulate the tenth Holon Principle:

---

[*] Holistic Logic suggests that the mind's contents reside in multi-dimensional reality.

HP10.   In a multi-dimensional whole, a change of any part affects all other parts.

This is like coloring one side of a crystal. Because the crystal is transparent, the hue permeates the entire crystal and colors all other sides. We see this effect sometimes in sport teams. The exchange of one player can change the character of the entire team, and we have a whole new ballgame. Most examples that we used for Holon principles earlier are not applicable to **HP9** and **HP10**, because they did not involve multi-dimensional wholes. Only the Self and the photon examples have multi-dimensional wholes. However these are not convincing examples for **HP10**, because we perceive both as having only two parts (mind & body, wave & particle). To verify that a change of one part affects *all* other parts, we would like to see more than just one other part affected. We will discuss examples for **HP9** and **HP10** for group entities in Chapter 5.

For easy reference, the Holon Principles are summarized on the next page.

HOLON PRINCIPLES

HP1. The number of dimensions of the whole exceeds that of its parts.

HP2. The whole and its parts are one, when viewed from the dimensional level of the whole.

HP3. The whole is invisible from the lower dimensional level of its parts.

HP4. The different aspects of the whole appear as separate parts, when viewed from the lower dimensional level of the parts

HP5. The reality of the whole is more significant than that of its parts.

HP6. Each part is itself a whole at a lower dimensional level.

HP7. The whole is immanent in each of its parts.

HP8. A change in a part corresponds to a change in the whole, and a change in the whole corresponds to a change in its parts.

HP9. No divisions and separations exist in multi-dimensional reality.

HP10. In a multi-dimensional whole, a change of any part affects all other parts.

The ten Holon Principles are a tool with which we can explore invisible multi-dimensional reality. It is invisible because your daytime consciousness does not perceive all its dimensions. You now have a better understanding of the significance of shifting your consciousness from one dimensional level to another. This does not mean that you can directly perceive multi-dimensional environments, but the Holon Principles serve as a logic system with which you can understand the nature of multi-dimensional reality – like having a map. They help you to become aware of true reality of which the physical world is only a limited projection.

The Holon Principles themselves form a holon that is an undivided whole. As I stated in the introduction, I experienced this whole directly, with all its aspects simultaneously evident. I can't describe this whole because of its multi-dimensional nature. So I've highlighted its different aspects and presented them as separate parts to fit into our customary thought pattern. In reality these aspects are not separate. With practice, you can obtain an innate understanding of Holistic Logic as one undivided unit.

We visualized the Holon Principles with the help of a crystal form, which is a three-dimensional example. However we have good reason to believe that these principles also apply to the entire invisible multi-dimensional environment. We can test the Holon Principles not only at our 3-D level with 2-D parts, as with the crystal, but also at lower dimensional levels, at 2-D and 1-D. In the description of **Holon Principle 6** (Each part is itself a whole at a lower dimensional level) we observed with the help of figures 1.16 and 1.17 that we can consider planes and lines as autonomous wholes at their own dimensional levels. They all form holons with their parts in their respective lower levels. For each of these holons one can check the first eight Holon Principles. The result is that the Holistic Logic applies in all cases. The two last Holon Principles apply only to multi-dimensional reality and they have been tested as later described in Chapter 5. We hope that more such scientific tests will be performed in the future.

If you feel up to it and like some mental exercise, verify the first eight Holon Principles for a holon in which a crystal plane is the whole and its edge lines are the parts of the plane. This is a holon that straddles the 2-D and the 1-D levels. Then repeat the same for the holon with a line as whole and the lines' points as the parts, covering 1-D and 0-D. (Hint: note for **HP8** that points can only change their positions). With this, you'll have tested the Holon Principles at three different levels:

1. Crystal: Whole = 3-D,   Parts = Planes = 2-D
2. Plane: Whole = 2-D,   Parts = Lines = 1-D
3. Line: Whole = 1-D,   Parts = points = 0-D

Additionally, the Holon Principles do a good job of describing holons that have wholes which are transcendent to three-dimensional parts, for instance photons, electrons, and the Self. We perceive their parts at our level of consciousness that is tuned to three-dimensional reality. Altogether, we have tested and confirmed the Holon Principles for four dimensional levels. This is the best we can do with the levels that are available to us.

Since the Holon Principles are true at all the dimensional levels that we can examine, it is reasonable to assume that they also apply to all multi-dimensional levels.

This kind of extrapolation is often practiced in science. We'll use our theory until something comes up that disproves it. **The application of Holistic Logic to the invisible multi-dimensional world leads naturally to conclusions that reconcile science and spirituality and that agree with the core concepts of world religions and philosophies.** I hope that this will become clear as you continue reading. Please note that I do not equate spirituality with religion. **Religions are human concepts of spirituality, not spirituality itself.**

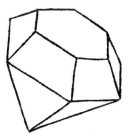

PART 2

THE

MULTI-DIMENSIONAL

REALITY

Chapter 4

The Nature of Space and Time

The distinction between past, present, and future is an illusion, although a persistent one.
ALBERT EINSTEIN

Albert Einstein's famous Theory of Relativity has dramatically changed scientists' understanding of space and time. In our everyday life we experience three-dimensional space and time as two separate concepts. We see objects that occupy space. We also experience time as a stream of sequential events, only one of which is real in the present. According to Albert Einstein's theory and a subsequent interpretation by the physicist Herman Minkowski, our concept of space and time does not agree with reality. Our three-dimensional space and our one-dimensional time are actually two aspects of a four-dimensional "super space," now called "spacetime." Our senses do not perceive spacetime directly, but its existence is well verified experimentally.

We cannot visualize the characteristics of spacetime. For instance, our space is "curved" in spacetime. We can think of a curved line or a curved plane, but we cannot imagine a curved 3-D space. However this is possible because spacetime is four-dimensional. The concept of spacetime is now an accepted integral part of modern physics. Checking our list of Holon Principles, we find that they agree with the scientific view of spacetime.

HP1. **The number of dimensions of the whole exceeds those of its individual parts.**
Correspondingly, the whole of spacetime has four dimensions, whereas its individual parts, space and time, have only three and one, respectively.

HP2. **The whole and its parts are one, when viewed from the dimensional level of the whole.**
Spacetime is also one with our space and time.

HP3. **The whole is invisible from the lower dimensional level of its parts.**
We cannot perceive spacetime from our lower-dimensional space and time.

HP4. **The different aspects of the whole appear as separate parts, when viewed from the lower dimensional level of the parts.**
Space and time appear as different parts of spacetime from our viewpoint.

HP5. **The reality of the whole is more significant than that of its parts.**
Scientists recognize spacetime as our "real" environment, because it explains actual phenomena that cannot be understood with our concept of separate space and time.

HP6. **Each part is itself a whole at a lower dimensional level.**
We experience our space as the unified whole of width, depth, and height, and our time is the whole of successive moments.

HP7. **The whole is immanent in each of its parts.**
Spacetime is within our space and our time, but transcends both.

HP8. **A change in a part corresponds to a change in the whole, and a change in the whole corresponds to a change in its parts.**
According the Einstein's General Theory of Relativity, any physical mass in 3-D space corresponds to a distortion of spacetime, and any distortion of spacetime corresponds to a physical mass in 3-D space. The mass in 3-D space represents a change compared with empty space. Also, 3-D space and time are indistinguishable in spacetime. Therefore the above sentence holds also true for time.

HP9. **No divisions and separations exist in multi-dimensional reality.**
While quantum theory supports this Holon Principle, relativity theory does not address this subject. A unified theory of quantum and relativity theories would probably provide an answer. Such a theory does not yet exist.

HP10. **In a multi-dimensional whole, a change of any part affects all other parts**. The statement for **HP9** also applies for **HP10**.

David Bohm, the prominent theoretical physicist mentioned earlier, thought of space and time as projections from a higher-dimensional reality, according to J. Briggs and D. Peat's book, *Looking Glass Universe*. And John Gribbin says in his *Search of Schroedinger's Cat*, "In this more fundamental type of reality, the distinction that we make between our 3-D space and time is meaningless."

Professor Stephen W. Hawking, one of the foremost theoretical physicists of our age, states in his book, *A Brief History of Time*, "We must accept that time is not completely separate from and independent of space, but is combined with it to form an object called spacetime." Also: "In reality, there is no real distinction between the space and time coordinates, just as there is no real difference between any two space coordinates."

Physicist and author Fritjof Capra describes in his book, *The Turning Point,* the difficulties we face in attempting to form an intuitive picture of the four-dimensional spacetime. This also applies to the physicists who have worked with it for decades and are thoroughly familiar with the mathematical formalism. To us, such a super space seems impossible to visualize. Yet we have to get used to the idea that it exists, and that we are living in it, here and now.

Let's again consider our perception of time. It does not exist as a sequential succession of events, but more like an additional space dimension, although even this statement must not be taken literally. In much the same way that we developed our concept of space, we have "invented" time, presumably so that we can focus on one thing at a time, rather than trying to deal with everything simultaneously. This allows us to experience life's events individually and more keenly, rather than passively watching them go by like a TV show. In this way we can cope with our challenges and rise above them. The disadvantage of this approach is that we do not see the true reality, and this makes us prone to mistakes. So let's try to get a better feeling of the true nature of time by using our imaginations and applying Holistic Logic. We think of time as a sequence of separate moments, events that occur one after another. These are best seen as parts of a whole that represents the more significant reality we want to understand (**HP5,** The reality of the whole is more significant than that of its parts).

Try not to imagine events one after the other and one at a time. Instead, imagine them next to each other, all visible simultaneously. Think of a trip you made. Recall the sites and events, and then imagine them all simultaneously. Do not force your brain to do this. It is not up to this task. Rather let go of brain thinking and let your inner Self do the visualization. If you do this correctly, it will feel good in your heart. It always feels good to be in touch with your inner Self. It is not important to actually accomplish this task. Rather, this exercise stimulates your mind to open up to higher reality. If you are musically inclined, listen to a symphony. After the performance, try to sense all movements simultaneously.

If you are adventurous enough, you may want to try this kind of exercise by considering your own life. Remember the events that come to your mind, and then let "your heart" hold them all simultaneously. You can accomplish this better when you love your Self, including the person you were in the past. Forgive yourself for anything that you may regret. Make a clear decision on how to handle that situation next time, and mentally send your regrets and apologies to whoever was involved, if this is appropriate. Then go on with your life. You will help no one by maintaining your feelings of guilt. On the contrary, by nursing your inner conflict, you will draw more conflicts to you, and you may affect others s well. With any of these examples, you can go even further and picture events in a sequence different than that which you remember.   This uncouples your limited linear sense of time and corresponds to the flexibility and nonlocality of multi-dimensional reality. This kind of exercise has practical value because it allows you to open your mind to the true reality that dwells within. Thus you will get to know yourself better and you will sharpen your intuitive understanding of the meaning of your life.

Our concept of time has only one dimension, it proceeds in one direction, from past to future. For us, events are lined up like beads on a string. However, in reality, events also occur outside of this string, adjacent to us. This is because the whole has more dimensions than its parts (**HP1**). In this case, time is one of the parts. We do not see the other dimensions, yet they affect us. Remember, in multi-dimensional reality the whole affects all its parts (**HP10**). Stephen Hawking wrote about this time-outside-our time in his bestseller, *A Brief History of Time*, and also in his latest book, *The Universe in a Nutshell*. He described this time outside our experience as "imaginary time" that has a clearly defined mathematical meaning. Similar to the experience of driving down a highway with landscape all around and clouds, birds, and airplanes above, we experience the immediate environment around us as the present event. Except for that which is in our visual range, we do not see the stretch that we have already traveled, nor do we see what is to come. Yet the entire route exists simultaneously at any moment, and the landscape stretches out into all directions endlessly.

Figure 2.1. Time is a path through a
multi-dimensional landscape

Similarly, we are not aware of events that exist around us in multi-dimensional reality. Our decisions in life are like turns we take at forks in the road, choosing a particular future course of events out of many possible ones. All other possible events still exist in the multi-dimensional environment as probabilities, but we did not choose to experience them. Instead of a landscape with roads, trees, houses, etc., the multi-dimensional landscape is composed of innumerable probable events. We experience only the ones closest to us. Multi-dimensional distance is not measured in miles or hours, but in probability of occurrence.

Intuitively, we may sense that there is more in our life's environment than what we see. We may feel depressed or uplifted for no obvious reason. We may have a foreboding or a joyful anticipation of events that are in our psychological vicinity but not obvious to us. Or we may step into a room and immediately sense its psychological climate – uplifting, depressing, or perhaps threatening. Each event we experience is an aspect of the greater fabric of life. Past, present, and future events are snapshots of one grand scene. We choose the pictures we take, depending on our interests. Other people traveling through the same territory may come back with quite different pictures. Past, present, and future all fold into one whole multi-dimensional reality. The whole and its parts are one (**HP2**). That whole is immanent in the present moment, because the whole is immanent in each of its parts (**HP7**). Thus focusing on the present moment, on the here and now, keeps us in touch with true reality.

Our present thoughts and actions affect our whole being, not only our present and future, but also our past. In multi-dimensional reality, a change of any part affects all other parts (**HP10**). Our inner self lives in multi-dimensional reality, where the past still exists, because past, present, and future are one. We only believe that they are separated from us because our waking consciousness lacks sufficient dimensions to experience the whole of what we call time. Immanently, we already understand the true nature of time because our inner self resides in multi-dimensionality, where time does not exist. It helps to keep this in mind when we attempt to overcome our misconceptions.

Since the multi-dimensional environment is immanent in us, we experience an inkling of it in our dreams. How else could we roam uninhibited through space and time when we dream? We may change places instantaneously and effortlessly, or we may be a child, and moments later an adult. We may also encounter friends and relatives who are no longer physically alive. Since the past continues to exist in multi-dimensional reality, our deceased companions are still here. Our inner multi-dimensional personality is free to go through its activities unrestrained by our daytime limitations. It is quite conscious at its own level, much more so than we are in our daytime activity. Try to remember what you already know immanently. Do not try to comprehend this with your rational mind. Your customary thinking cannot grasp multi-dimensional reality. Perceive it with your heart.

We can awaken to multi-dimensional reality and experience it even while living physically; short of that, we can simply become accustomed to its truth, as we have become accustomed to the laws of nature that seemed mysterious at one time. In the Middle Ages it must have been difficult for people to accept that the world was a globe orbiting the sun.

Eventually, humankind will take it for granted that time does not exist as a sequence of moments lined up one after the other. Only the present is real, charged with an incredible variety of possible events that occupy a multi-dimensional world. We are only tuning into a tiny portion of it, like selecting one TV channel out of an untold number. What we call past and future are our minds' concepts based on selective memory and anticipation, they are not the living reality. Our present frame of mind simply does not have the capacity to comprehend all the other events, just as we cannot watch all TV channels simultaneously.

Chapter 5

Group Entities

We know now that wholes are invisible from the lower dimensional level of their parts (**HP3**). We also know that the different aspects of a whole appear as separate parts in the lower dimensional level of the parts (**HP4**). Yet, although their mutual whole is not directly visible from the parts' level, we still can see that the parts belong together, that they represent the same category or species. For instance, all humans are parts of a common whole, but we usually don't think of the whole of humankind as an individual autonomous entity in multi-dimensional reality. Holistic Logic postulates that the whole of all humans exists as an autonomous multi-dimensional entity. It has more dimensions than any individual (**HP1**). Therefore it is transcendent to us and we can't see it (**HP3**). Let's call the transcendent whole of humanity 'Humankind-Entity'.

Humankind-Entity dwells in multi-dimensional reality where our limited concepts of space and time are not valid. What we perceive as individuals are different aspects of the same enormous multi-dimensional entity (**HP4**, The different aspects of the whole appear as separate parts, when viewed from the lower dimensional level of the parts). These aspects are actually not separated in the multi-dimensional Humankind-Entity. Also, because our concept of sequential time does not exist at the multi-dimensional level, all people who ever lived and who ever will live are united in Humankind-Entity, which encompasses the characteristics and capabilities of all these humans. The whole and its parts are one. Humankind-Entity is more intelligent than the smartest people throughout history combined, because they are but limited aspects of it.

From its exalted multi-dimensional environment, Humankind-Entity perceives interrelationships and potentials that are quite beyond our imaginations. Humankind-Entity has incredible vitality and power. Some people might think that Humankind-Entity is not real because it does not exist physically. This type of thinking is like that of Plato's cave dwellers giving more credibility to shadows rather than to true reality.

Figure 2.2. Humankind-Entity Holon

Humankind-Entity is immanent in all of us. (The whole is immanent in each of its parts, **HP7**). Therefore we can identify some of Humankind-Entity's characteristics and desires that we all have in common. For instance, we all pursue our own interests. We look out for our survival, and we follow what we believe is good for us. Humankind-Entity does the same on its level of existence. Since Humankind-Entity is one with us, it then follows that it is in our self-interest to promote the interests of the whole of Humankind-Entity.

We can say that your hand moves in response to impulses from your nervous system. These, in turn, were initiated by your decision to move your hand. In other words, the hand moves instinctively, on impulse, or spontaneously. This instinct is nothing less than the message that your immanent whole is sending to your parts, in this case to your hand. Your hand can trust its instincts because you are vitally interested in its welfare. The same holds true for your relationship with Humankind-Entity, only we are given much more leeway to follow our individual desires.

Responding to Humankind-Entity's interests does not impair our freedom; on the contrary. Since Humankind-Entity is immanent in us, we act with our heart's desire. Humankind-Entity is our very essence, our root source. To give expression to it means to be truly human. Thus we unfold our innermost potential. To be free means that we can do what we want, and ideally, we want to express our innermost desires, the inner call of Humankind-Entity. Humankind-Entity's will is our immanent will. There is no conflict.

Yet we are not perfect, and we may not listen to our hearts. We pursue goals that deviate from what is good for us and for humanity. Free will is cosmic law. We can do whatever we want, even go against humanity's interests. The more we do this, the more we uncouple our minds from our hearts, and thus from Humankind-Entity, our inner source. If we do this long enough, we lose the feel for what is good for our inner Self, and we lose the warm and secure feeling of being centered within ourselves, no matter how successful we may be in our external pursuits.

Humanity now faces this problem on a global scale. Life is becoming increasingly complicated. Things do not fall into place naturally, as they do when thoughts and actions are in line with the perfect inner harmony of

Humankind-Entity, which experiences no inner divisions at that level. No division and separation exists in multi-dimensional reality (**HP9**). Humanity-Entity lives in a state of paradise. The whole and its parts are one, when viewed from the dimensional level of the whole (**HP2**).

When Adam ate the allegorical apple from the tree of knowledge, he allowed his mind to think independently of his heart. Would a loving God create us with a thirst for knowledge and then throw us out when we pursue it? Actually, making the mind independent of pure instinct was an evolutionary step forward. It provided humankind with additional freedom to think and to reflect on itself. Without this breakthrough we would have no analytical skill, no science, no technology, and no philosophy. It is only when we let the mind run away with itself, forgetting to check with the heart, that trouble looms. Now that we have tested our freedom to do whatever we want with the power of independent thought, and now that we are becoming aware of where it can lead us if we are not careful, it is time for the next evolutionary step. It is time to understand the inner workings of reality and to accept our responsibility to think and act accordingly.

Humankind-Entity is aware of our thoughts, because its consciousness includes the consciousness of each individual person. (**HP2**, The whole and its parts are one, when viewed from the dimensional level of the whole). It implements its own decisions in communion with us, as we implement our decisions in communion with our minds and bodies. As we pursue our lives, we add our personal experience to the essence of humanity because any part's change affects its whole (**HP8**). Thus we give something back. Our relationship with Humankind-Entity is a two-way street. Our individual experiences are part of a "data base" for Humankind-Entity to use for its evolution.

Our experience is also Humankind-Entity's experience. It depends on us, as we depend on our hands. Since any person's change means a change in Humankind-Entity, it also means an immanent change in all other humans (**HP10**). Such subtle but real interchanges between people are more obvious and more immediate in close groups because groups form multi-dimensional wholes of their own on a more intimate scale. However, the same mechanism is at work on the grand scale of all humanity. Do your own thoughts and actions affect everyone, not just yourself? They do indeed! Because of our inner interdependence, we carry responsibility for others as well as for ourselves, whether we are aware of it or not. A drug abuser hurts us all, and the positive efforts of others elevate all of society.

As a useful exercise, give yourself fifteen undisturbed minutes. Sit quietly and imagine yourself as an integral part of Humankind-Entity, as if you are an integral plane of a crystal. This means opening your heart. You will find that you can do this only when you love humanity, when you love people, regardless of who they are. This is so because we can only be in harmony with ourselves when we are in harmony with our own core, which is Humankind-Entity immanent in us.

This knowledge greatly affects how we think and act. Through the ages, poets and philosophers have given us these insights, yet we may have considered them nice, idealistic thoughts that are not necessarily realistic. Now we have arrived at these conclusions logically, corroborated by modern scientific thought. This is reality. We are beginning to see how we can improve humanity's lot, how we can all contribute to its evolution.

The group-entity concept is not new. As mentioned earlier, Plato described transcendent, invisible "forms" that cause physical manifestations in our world. The Swiss psychologist Carl G. Jung (1875-1961) concluded that humans share one collective unconscious that lies deeper than the unconscious of each individual. He observed that the same basic symbols, myths, and fairy tales can be found in widely separated cultures, even though no contacts could have occurred between them. Such themes and symbols also appear in dreams. So there must be an inner connection.

Jung called these thought patterns "archetypes." Typical archetypes are "hero," "mother," and "shadow." Jung said that an individual's psyche is not only her personal, individual concern, but is also unconsciously shared with all other people. Sigmund Freud expressed a similar opinion. Carl Jung thought that the experiences of ancestors accumulate as archetypes in the collective unconscious of humankind. Our Holistic Logic concept of the Humankind-Entity corresponds to Carl Jung's collective unconscious. Jung's archetype thought patterns are in Humankind-Entity's consciousness, therefore they are immanent in us as instinctive inclinations.

Biologists view animal societies as entities, especially colonies of insects such as bees, wasps, ants, and termites. The British biologist Rupert Sheldrake has generated much interest in this subject. He suggests group "fields" that exist beyond our physical reality. He calls them "morphogenetic fields," or "m-fields." They contain all information needed to support the growth and survival of the species, much like the holistic group-entity concept postulated here.

Sheldrake cites many convincing examples of these transcendent entities. He describes, for instance, how beehives are organized with an intelligence that far exceeds the capacity of an individual bee. Honeybees maintain the internal temperatures of their nests within one or two degrees from spring through fall. They do this by carefully sealing off all uncontrolled drafts, and warming the interiors with their body heat by huddling together, more or less as needed. In hot weather, they carry water into their nests, spread it out, and enhance its cooling evaporation by fanning air over the water with their wings. Another of Sheldrake's examples is the mounds made by compass termites in Australia. These tall mounds are very narrow in one direction, but broad in the other, so that they are least exposed to the sun's intense noon radiation. These impressive capabilities can only be understood if a unified group intelligence guides its individuals.

Sheldrake also reports what appears to be mysterious communication between members of a species. The communication occurs between individuals that are too far separated for direct contact. He explains this phenomenon as what he calls "morphic resonance." By this he means that individuals resonate their information with the transcendent collective m-field, which in turn resonates with other members separated by space and time. Sheldrake's m-fields correspond to our multi-dimensional group-entities, and his morphic resonance corresponds to Holon Principle **HP10** (In a multi-dimensional whole, a change of any part affects all other parts).

The most widely known anecdotal evidence of communication between group members via their common group-entity is what is called the "hundredth monkey effect." The biologist Lyall Watson reported it in his 1970 book *Lifetide.* Watson wrote that this event occurred on a Japanese island where researchers had fed sweet potatoes to Macaca monkeys. This was a new, unknown staple for the monkeys. They liked the potatoes, but they did not like the beach sand that covered them. One monkey started to wash the potatoes in the ocean. This also added a desirable salty taste. After a certain number of monkeys had copied this action, it was suddenly and spontaneously practiced by the entire community, as if a critical mass of potato-washing monkeys triggered this behavior in all their group members. Shortly thereafter, according to the report, even monkeys on other islands began to practice the potato washing procedure, although there was no communication between the islands.

The above anecdote does not represent scientific evidence, however laboratory experiments appear to confirm 'nonlocal' communication between members of a group via their common whole, corresponding to **HP10**. Sheldrake reports in his book, *The Presence of the Past,* on an experiment with rats. The rats had been placed individually into a maze, and the time it took the rats to find their way out was measured. Later rat generations performed this task successively faster. As more rats had become familiar with the maze, even untrained, genetically unrelated rats showed higher learning speeds.

Similar effects have been observed even with inanimate objects, according to Sheldrake. Mineralogists have found that crystals are often very difficult to grow initially when using a new substance. Once grown in one place, however, the same crystallization can be replicated more and more easily, even on other continents. This appears to demonstrate a nonlocal connection between the crystals via a common multi-dimensional whole. Other examples of group-entities include flocks of birds, migrating animal herds, and schools of fish behaving like single units.

Sheldrake's hypothesis of morphic resonance (corresponding to **Holon Principle 10**) has also been tested with humans. One test involved Japanese nursery rhymes. British and American groups who could not speak Japanese were given two rhymes, a traditional rhyme known to virtually every Japanese, and another nonsensical rhyme composed for the test. After chanting each of them a given number of times, participants recalled the traditional rhyme significantly more accurately than the nonsensical one. Similar tests were conducted in the Hebrew and Persian languages, with Russian typewriter keyboards, and with Morse code. Results showed invariably that people who had never been exposed to the correct versions could learn them more easily than the false equivalents.

Based on Holistic Logic and the cited supporting information, we will assume that **group entities exist, not only for humanity, but also for all species.** All such entities are multi-dimensional and therefore invisible to us, yet from their own viewpoint they are more real than their individual members. The Holon Principles describe how the group-entities interact with their members and with the universe.

Chapter 6

The Cosmic Holarchy

THE HOLARCHY

Holistic Logic helps us to understand the universe's inner composition and our own position in it. It gives us a simple map to navigate in multi-dimensional reality. This reality appears rather complicated to us, because we do not see it. Yet it boils down to one overwhelmingly simple truth: **We Are All One, from top to bottom, from left to right, everywhere.** Holistic Logic tells us that the whole unites all its parts into one undivided entity. Other sources give us the same message, as we shall discuss.

In Chapter 5 we saw how Holistic Logic leads us to the conclusion that group-entities exist for animal species, invisible to us in multi-dimensional space. To be logically consistent, we must also assume that plants have their species-entities. Holistic Logic applies to all wholes and their parts, and everything in the universe is organized into wholes and parts, living beings as well as what we call inanimate matter. Therefore it is logical that invisible transcendent group-entities exist also for so-called inanimate categories, such as chemical elements and continents. All these group entities are themselves parts of even higher order wholes, forming holons of unimaginable greatness.

We can consider the planet Earth a super entity. According to Holistic Logic, the unifying whole of the Earth exists in multi-dimensional reality. Since Earth includes all the characteristics of its parts, it is as alive as we are, with its own survival-interest. (**HP3, the whole and its parts are one, when viewed from the dimensional level of the whole**). According to Fritjof Capra in *The Turning Point*, a growing number of scientists are accepting this view of Earth's nature. Capra refers to the chemist James Lovelock and the microbiologist Lynn Margulis, who suggest that many phenomena within the Earth's biosphere can be understood only if the planet as a whole is regarded as a single living organism. Yet, even the Earth is only a relatively minute spec in the whole universe, and it is a holistic part of ever grander multi-dimensional entities: our solar system, our galaxy, and beyond.

Finally, an ultimate entity exists that encompasses all that is, visible and invisible. We shall call it "All-Entity." This entity has unlimited dimensions, and everything that exists is one of Its aspects seen from a lower order. Everything whatsoever is Its integral part. All-Entity unites everything in a single, undivided whole.

Before we proceed, it is beneficial to understand the relationship between holons that are stacked on top of each other in a hierarchy of holons, what Koestler called a "holarchy." Figure 2.3a shows a schematic diagram of a holarchy with three dimensional levels A, B, C. The A-Entity is the whole of three B-Entities, and the B-Entities are the wholes of their respective C-parts. A-Entity forms a holon with its three parts B, and each B-Entity forms a holon with its corresponding C-parts on the next lower level.

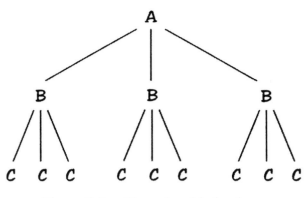

Figure 2.3a. Three-level holarchy.

Since the Cs are parts of their wholes B, and the Bs are parts of A, the Cs are also parts of A. Therefore the whole A at the top and the C's in the bottom row also form a holon with each other (figure 2.3b). This A-to-C holon is one like any other as discussed in Part 1, and all Holon Principles, **HP1** through **HP10**, apply between the levels A and C, as if level B did not exist in between.

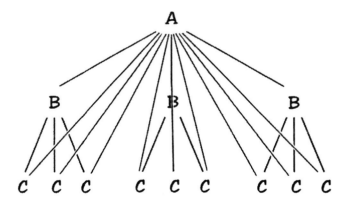

Figure 2.3b. Holarchy across two levels.

One can use the same logic repeatedly and conclude that there can be countless levels between a whole and its parts, for instance for the planet Earth and all its individual creatures. The Holon Principles still apply directly between the multi-dimensional Earth-Entity and an ant, or a raindrop.

Take for instance **HP1**, the whole has more dimensions than each of its parts. In Figure 2.3a, the top A-entity has more dimensions than each of the C-parts at the bottom, because if A has more dimensions than B, and B has more dimensions than C, then A has more dimensions than C. It does not matter how many levels are stacked up. The Holon Principle still applies because the logic is valid for any number of steps simultaneously. This makes things easy for us. We do not have to worry about how many levels are between a whole and its parts, Holistic Logic describes their mutual relationship. For instance, we can tell about the interplay between Humankind-Entity and individual humans without exactly knowing the subdivisions in between, such as different races, countries, or different psychological profiles. These form sub-holons of their own without interfering with the overall humankind holon of which they are parts. They don't interfere because Humankind-Entity is one with all its parts, from the whole's point of view (**HP2**), regardless of whether we, as parts, perceive subdivisions from our viewpoint. A holarchy exists only from the parts' points of view, not from that of the whole. The fact that the parts have fewer dimensions creates the impression of subsets in the whole where none actually exist from the multi-dimensional view of the whole.

Think of what this means for your relationship with All-Entity! According to **HP2**, you are one with All-Entity as seen from All-Entity's point of view. No separation exists between All-Entity and you. Since All-

Entity has infinitely more dimensions than we mortals, It's viewpoint is most significant (**HP5, the reality of the whole is more significant than that of its parts**). Any notion that you are separated from All-Entity is simply false. You only think this way because you do not see All-Entity with your eyes (**HP3**).

Humankind's acceptance of this truth would cause a quantum advance in its evolution. The time for it is NOW. Throughout history, enlightened individuals walked the Earth. They were conscious of their oneness with the All, even as they were living in their physical bodies. They taught us that we can awaken to the ultimate reality of our unity with All-Entity during physical life. Somehow, this message has been diluted. Western religions tell us to behave well so that we will be accepted into heaven. We are even told to fear God, which emphasizes our sense of separation. Some feel that our distance to God is so great that we need an advocate to speak for us. We are not talking about this kind of god here. We are talking about the Whole of All-That-Is. It embraces everything, rejecting nothing and no one. That is our definition. It is also the definition of unconditional Love. All-Entity cannot possibly reject anything. To do so, it would have to tear Itself apart. This is impossible, because nothing can be apart from the whole of everything, or it would not be the whole of everything. All parts together **are** All-Entity from the viewpoint that has the most significant reality.

We will refer repeatedly to All-Entity and God in this book, and it is appropriate to clarify how these terms will be used. The definition of All-Entity has already been stated. The term "God" has different connotations depending on an individual's cultural background. Generally, God is thought of as the highest entity of all. In this sense, the terms God and All-Entity are synonymous. However, religious concepts of God usually differ from the concept of All-Entity in that they attribute human qualities to God, depicting Him as God the father and as a God who could be angry and evict Adam and Eve from Paradise. In our concept of All-Entity, these ideas have only allegorical meaning and are misleading when taken literally. All-Entity has no personality because this would imply a human characteristic and thus a lower dimension. Yet, we will continue to use the term God for All-Entity in the book occasionally.

ALL-ENTITY

All-Entity unifies all that exists into one seamless, harmonious Being (**HP2**). All-Entity is a "Living Being," because It includes all living beings. All-Entity is life's essence, pure consciousness. Its human aspects are only a very small part of It. To imagine All-Entity in human terms is misleading. All-Entity has no individuality, if we define individuality as differing from others. No others exist at that level. As an undivided and unified entity, All-Entity is the pure potential of unlimited possibilities, none of which are expressed at that level. This is why All-Entity must create. Can you imagine being full of ideas, love, and vitality, and sitting at home doing nothing? We can identify with this feeling, because All-Entity is immanent in us.

Perhaps this need for expression originated the "Big Bang," the birth of the universe, and the evolution of all its parts. All-Entity's unlimited potential acts like a pressure overload seeking release. Physicists see the Big Bang as a purely physical event. However, holistically, we must assume that it is vastly multi-dimensional. We should also keep in mind that time does not exist in multi-dimensional reality. Everything occurs simultaneously, as discussed before. Just as multi-dimensional reality is nonlocal in terms of space, so it is nontemporal in terms of time. The Big Bang is still occurring in the ever present multi-dimensional NOW while we live in a "trickle-down" reality at some lower multi-dimensional strata. As astronomers peer through ever more powerful telescopes into cosmic events seemingly billions of years past, they are approaching the physical aspect of that primeval region. This is as close to God as we can get with our eyes, but we are already intimately closer in our hearts. No spatial distance exists in nonlocal multi-dimensional reality. **This is why multi-dimensionality is nonlocal; All-Entity is immanent in everything, and everything is one in All-Entity. Thus no separation exists between anything in multi-dimensional reality.**

As life itself, All-Entity evolves continually (**HP8**, any change in a part corresponds to a change in the whole, and a change in the whole corresponds to a change in its parts). We expect perfection at the cosmic holarchy's top, but perfection does not imply a state beyond further development. That would be the end of all life, because no incentive for further change would exist. Instead, the perfection lies in the vibrant process of life's evolution itself.

We identify All-Entity with unconditional Love. We also say that It is the life essence, that It is pure consciousness. Add to this ultimate joy, peace, intelligence, power and many more absolutes of one kind or another. We think of them as different characteristics, yet they are all one in All-Entity (**HP2**). Picture this as we experience our three-dimensional space as one cohesive environment, even though it has three independent dimensions with different characteristics: width, depth, and height. There is no conflict because

All-Entity is the ultimate of all different characteristics simultaneously.

As the grandest Whole there is, All-Entity forms the Supreme Holon with all that exists, visible and invisible. We have now come to the great mystery of the universe. Its total entity is a three-in-one unit. It consists of the Whole of everything, of all its parts, and of the Holon connecting them. The Christian Church calls this the Holy Trinity, the doctrine that God exists as three-in-one. In holistic terms, the **Father** is the Whole, the **Son** the totality of the parts (everything that comes from the Whole), and the **Holy Spirit** is the Holon that combines both together into One. Similarly, in Hinduism, Trimurti unites the gods Brahma, Vishnu, and Shiva, who represent the three aspects of the Supreme Being. We can even go into the Andes and discover what the ancient Incas tell us about their three-in-one cosmic system. It all makes holistic logical sense.

As the whole of everything, All-Entity is immanent in everything. Thus everything in the universe is comprised of this trinity, and we find holons everywhere. You are a holon, "made in His image," having body, mind, and soul. **Since All-Entity is the essence of life and immanent in everything, even that which we consider dead matter, such as rock, is immanently conscious.** Some form of consciousness is in every atom. Our inability to sense life in "dead matter" does not mean that it is not there. We already understand that we cannot depend on our senses to perceive true reality. We know that molecules, atoms, and subatomic parts are very active indeed. We may consider this activity a form of life; as a part of All-Entity, which is life's essence, it cannot be otherwise. Native Americans have always been close to this understanding. We have good reason to appreciate that their tradition has kept these ideas alive. David Bohm also thought that life is implicit in what we call inanimate matter. Philosophers have made similar statements in the past.

By transcending everything in the universe, All-Entity resolves all differences between entities anywhere in the universe. Any opposites are just different aspects of a whole that exists undivided and harmoniously at a higher level. The differences are resolved when we raise our consciousness enough to see the other aspects of a situation. As the author Dr. Wayne Dyer says, "there's a spiritual solution to every problem."

If we could see multi-dimensional reality at different dimensional levels, descending down the cosmic holarchy, reality would appear increasingly differentiated into a multiplicity of ever more specialized parts. Still, each part represents an aspect of All-Entity. You are one, as is the wind, an earthquake, a Galaxy, the termite nibbling at your house, even the terrorist flying a Boeing 767 into the World Trade Center (more on this later).

Some of you may find it difficult to accept that you are so intimate with the highest Entity of the universe, in spite of your "sins." All your life you have been told otherwise, making you feel unworthy of such a close relationship. From our limited perception, it was easy to accept those teachings and feel separated from All-Entity. But now you understand why. Your mind grasps only a few of All-Entity's dimensions, yet you are an integral aspect of It, like one surface of a multifaceted crystal, or one color out of white light. White light could not be white without all its colors. All-Entity could not be All-Entity without you. Not one iota could be cast off. **There is no place away from All-Entity.**

All-Entity includes all human dimensions, but harbors no limiting notions such as wrath, revenge, and damnation, as some religions maintain. How can All-Entity condemn a sinner, when that person is All-Entity's own integral part? This would be as if you deliberately injured yourself. The whole and its parts are one.

All-Entity is our innermost source. As our own inner core, It is on intimate terms with us, whether we acknowledge this or not. All-Entity knows our every thought, including the most private ones, because our consciousness is part of All-Entity's consciousness. While All-Entity participates in our thoughts, It leaves us free to think and do whatever we want. Through us, All-Entity experiences Its own myriad possibilities.

By being all-inclusive and all-accepting, All-Entity is unconditional Love. When we love someone, we do not create love, rather we draw on the inexhaustible source within us. The more we do this, the more we experience love in return because we widen the inner channel to its source. In other words, the more we think and act like All-Entity, the more we *are* All-Entity, our own ultimate Self. With this attitude come quite a few "fringe benefits." The more holistically we think, the more we experience this divine Love. Conversely, the less tolerant we are and the fewer dimensions we accept, the more we obstruct our inner connection to the Love within us. Thus we feel separated, because we have fewer dimensions with which to experience All-Entity. All-Entity does not withdraw Its Love, rather we withdraw ourselves from It.

Since we are one with All-Entity, we are immortal. Our Self exists in timeless multi-dimensional reality, and timelessness is endless. Our physical bodies obey time, but our concept of time is not valid in true reality. While in the body, we forget who we really are. This enables us to gain life experience not possible otherwise. The reduced scope of our consciousness allows us to focus on specific ventures. When your body dies, your Self maintains its own individuality in the multi-dimensional domain. There is no conflict between being merged with All-Entity, and simultaneously being an individual aspect of It. Holistic Logic explains this. The whole is one while its aspects appear separate at their own level. The difference is in the viewpoint, not the true reality.

All-Entity has the potential of unlimited dimensions. It has no need to wipe out the subset of an individual. Quite the opposite, All-Entity seeks each individual's experience. Whatever we experience, All-Entity experiences through us, because It is one with us. This is how All-Entity creates Its Own experience.

Chapter 7

Who Are We?

Everything is part of a greater whole, with the exception of All-Entity, the ultimate whole. Our minds and our bodies are parts of our whole Selves, and our Selves must belong to an even greater whole. This greater whole must be immanent in us, inside and transcendent to us and beyond our Self's dimensions. **HP7** tells us: the whole is immanent in each of its parts. This immanent whole has more dimensions than our Self. It encompasses more of All-Entity's dimensions. In this sense, it is closer to and more connected with All-Entity. We have a name for this whole. We call it the soul. Your soul is invisible to your Self because any whole is invisible from the lower dimensional level of its parts (**HP3**). Therefore, you only have a vague idea about the true nature of your soul. Most Christians and Jews believe that the soul is the immortal part of a person that seeks communion with God in the afterlife. Islam has a similar concept of the soul. Most Eastern religions consider the soul the essence of the individual. They believe that it goes through many cycles of physical reincarnation until it is purified and reunited with God.

When we use Holistic Logic, our concept of the nature of the soul differs from what traditional world religions and philosophies espouse. Despite this difference, however, our concept also embraces many similarities, and in effect, serves to unify the beliefs of these various religions. Firstly, the soul is always an integral part of All-Entity and can never be separated. All-Entity would not be whole without all its parts. We may experience a feeling of separation because we cannot see All-Entity, and because of our erroneous thinking and acting. But we are never separated from All-Entity, no matter what we think and do.   In order to experience All-Entity's presence, we must align our minds to Its dimensions; we must tune into Its channel. The 'broadcast" is always there, but our attention is diverted by the onslaught of other channels, most of which are not helpful.

Now that we have reached a certain overview of the cosmic order, the question remains, where exactly do we fit in?   How do we relate to our environment in this holarchy?   Perhaps more to the point: who are we? Imagine yourself on the holarchy once more. Begin with your organs and see how they are each part of your body. In turn, your mind and your body are parts of your Self. The Self is a part of your soul. Now, where or who are the other parts of your soul? If the soul is a whole of which you are a part, there must be other parts, besides your Self, that belong to the same soul. Remember our diagram of the crystal (Fig. 1.7). If the crystal represents your soul and one of the planes is your Self, then it follows that the other planes must be other Selves, like yours, that exist in different dimensions of the same multi-dimensional entity. In other words, your soul forms a holon with many Selves as its parts, one of which is your own Self (Fig 2.4). The different Selves do not see each other, because they exist in different dimensions. (Please note that we use the term Self with a capital S for the invisible transcendent whole of mind and body, however self with a small s means the self of an individual that we are aware of in our present reality).

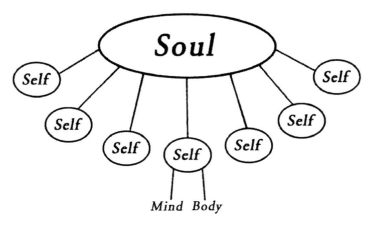

Figure 2.4 The soul is a whole with many selves
as its parts.

Our 2D creatures that live on the crystal plane A in figure 2.5 cannot see their companions in the other planes, because they do not coincide with the world of the A-plane creatures.   The other planes are transcendent to plane A, which means they are beyond the experience of the 2Ds of plane A.   Also, plane A is transcendent to the 2Ds in each of the other planes. So are we not aware of the other selves that belong to our soul, and the others are not aware of us. Do not think of your companion selves as strangers. They represent other aspects of your soul. We could call them soul mates.   You may feel uncomfortable with the concept of parallel selves if you are not familiar with it, even though it follows logically from the Holon Principles.   However, other sources discussed in Chapter 9 support this concept.

Figure 2.5   Crystal with 2Ds on different planes.

Remember now that time does not exist in multidimensional reality. We treat episodes outside our present **as if** they fall into different time periods. We do this because otherwise we would be hopelessly overloaded with a mass of impressions. So it seems to us that the other Selves of our soul lived at different times in the past and will do so in the future. This is how the concept of reincarnation must have originated. As mentioned in Chapter 2, some people, especially children, remember that they had lived before in previous lives. Dr. Stevenson's team has investigated thousands of such cases. We heard about the boy who remembered that he was a Turkish bandit in a former life and shot himself when he was cornered, and that an older person was able to confirm his story.

Another case in Dr. Stevenson's records concerned a Beirut toddler who persistently picked up the phone and tried to reach "Leila." No one in her family knew an individual by that name. As the child grew older, she explained in detail that she had been a Lebanese mother of three, and that she had died during heart surgery. She also provided enough information that her parents were able to locate the girl's former family. These family members confirmed how the mother of three had died, and that in her last days she had desperately tried to reach her daughter Leila on the phone. The Beirut girl had also remembered thirteen of her former relatives by name, and during a later visit she addressed them correctly without having been introduced. She also asked whether her daughters had received her jewelry as she had requested on her deathbed, a detail that only the relatives of the deceased woman knew.

Naturally, individuals who remember their other incarnations do so within our customary perception of sequential time. However in reality, these incarnations exist simultaneously in multi-dimensional reality as other parts of our soul.

Take "time" out now and relax. Imagine yourself as an integral part of a much greater spiritual entity that is your soul. It is immanent in you and has a more significant reality than you (**HP5**). It is your essence. Having its multi-dimensional vantage point, your soul has extraordinary capabilities. It supports many incarnations who are your closest soul mates. They all live simultaneously and they affect your life, as you unknowingly affect theirs. In a multi-dimensional whole, a change of any part affects all other parts (**HP10**). So send them your love. It will make them feel better and it will elevate your joint soul. This in turn makes you feel better. It also expands your mind into multi-dimensional reality.

In the metaphor of figure 2.5, your soul can see all sides of the crystal and can be in touch with its parts on different planes. In fact, the soul lives in all planes simultaneously and immanently, because it is one with all its parts. Perhaps you want to imagine your soul as an octopus inside the crystal form, stretching its tentacles out onto the different surface planes. Wherever a tentacle touches a plane, it shows up there as a 2D creature that cannot see its "octopus soul," because the soul is transcendent.

Figure 2.6   3-D octopus-soul creating 2-D creatures

Your soul has enough dimensions to experience all its incarnations simultaneously, without missing a beat. In other words, your soul is an incredibly capable super-human entity with divine qualities. It has perfect memory, because it continues to experience all its incarnations even though they existed centuries ago in linear time. The soul also has precognition, because it already lives in what we perceive as the future. And it has the combined experience of all its incarnations, past, present and future, in our terms. You have good reason to listen to your soul. **According to Holistic Logic, the Eastern concept of souls progressing from one body to another is misleading. It would be more appropriate to call them co-incarnations rather than re-incarnations.**

We do not become a soul when we die. We are a soul now, but we experience only one aspect of it. We also can never lose our soul, as some religions claim, because the whole and its parts are one (**HP2**). Since the soul is immanent in each of its Selves, each Self refers to "my soul," as if it belongs to only that particular Self. Actually, this is like talking about "my family," "my country" or "my mother," something or someone shared with others.

You can hardly imagine your soul's extraordinary grandeur. Its experience and intelligence surpasses that of all its incarnations, since any whole is more than its parts. Each self's consciousness is a part of the soul's consciousness. Thus the soul participates in the experience of all its incarnations. It can compare experiences of its incarnations "across the board" and draw useful conclusions.

Life pulses between the whole and its parts in both directions. A change in a part corresponds to a change in the whole, and a change in the whole corresponds to a change in its parts (**HP8**). The soul expresses itself through its incarnations to implement and experience its potential in the physical world. This is the soul's way of experiencing its own inner resources as we experience ours by acting in our environment. In return, the Selves provide the "data base" of life experiences for the soul. The soul is the life source for all its incarnations. It arranges broad areas of activities for them and allows them to freely pursue their own goals and follies. From the soul's viewpoint, the lessons learned by the selves through "bad" experiences are perhaps most valuable. Failures do not exist in multi-dimensional reality because every experience is an evolutionary gain. The emotional effect of all experiences dwells in the soul and therefore is immanent in all its Selves. This provides a framework of instincts and inclinations on which the Selves develop their individual characters.

Your soul, as magnificent as it already is, is a part of an even greater multi-dimensional entity, and that entity is a part of a grander one yet, and so on up to All-Entity. Figure 2.7 illustrates some of these super-entities of which you are a part. We see physical aspects of them in our world, but their multi-dimensional entities are way beyond our capability to imagine. Yet, since we belong to their realm and since we are their parts, they are immanent in all of us at ever deeper levels of our psyches. They make up the foundation of who we are. They are our inner conduit to life.

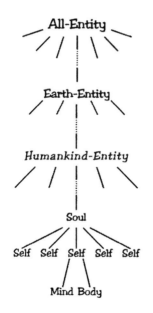

Figure 2.7. The human psyche.

Figure 2.7 is a highly simplified diagram that demonstrates this basic concept. At the bottom is the reality you know, your mind and body. By "mind" I mean that part of your consciousness that you experience when living in a body. It is your ego-consciousness, where the word "ego" has no negative connotation. For this discussion, the ego is simply that limited aspect of your self with which you identify while physically alive.

To facilitate understanding, the categories in Fig. 2.7 are shown as separate. This way our minds can more easily picture the mutual relationships and influences of different dimensional levels in the universe. This gives us an idea of how we fit into this grand scheme. In reality, however, the different levels are all merged into one whole, as seen from the dimensional level of All-Entity (**HP2**). The holarchy exists only from our point of view as parts, because we lack the dimensions to perceive the unity of all (**HP1**). For instance, it is impossible to say where the Self stops and the soul starts – no dividing line exists. We should become accustomed to the idea that we cannot delegate multi-dimensional reality into neat separate compartments. To understand multi-dimensional reality, we must rely more on the heart's perception rather than on analytical thinking. **Our analytical minds are accustomed to focusing on detail and parts and are not well suited for holistic perception.**

All-Entity is the essence of everything. Therefore It is also the essence of consciousness. Since the whole is immanent in its parts, all the entities noted in Figure 2.7 are conscious. The lower an entity is on the holarchy, the smaller the scope of its consciousness. Your mind is less aware than your inner Self. A Self is less aware than the soul, etc. Since a part's consciousness is smaller than that of the whole, the part cannot cover the whole's consciousness. Thus the whole is invisible from the lower dimensional level of its parts (**HP3**). So it follows that our minds are unaware of our inner Self's consciousness.

The Self is always conscious, day and night. Its range of activities is far greater than that of the ego. We get glimpses of the actions of our inner Self in our dreams but we don't understand them because we don't see the whole picture, and we don't understand the multi-dimensional environment.

We can assume that our living body also has its own unique consciousness. We concluded earlier that everything is conscious. Your Self's consciousness is the unified whole of mind and body-consciousness. So talk to your body with compassion. It may not understand English, but it certainly gets the emotional message you express. It senses your emotions even when you don't verbalize them. Your thoughts and emotions affect your body's wellness according to **HP10**: in a multi-dimensional whole, a change of any part affects all other parts. Faith healing can work for those who believe in it.

All entities shown above the soul in figure 2.7 are immanent in it. Therefore they are also immanent in your Self, your mind, and your body. Humankind-Entity is immanent in you, with its collective intelligence, experience, and challenges. We are not so much aware of Earth-Entity's immanence, because the Earth environment is the only one we are experiencing. We do not experience our uniqueness as Earthlings because we lack comparisons. And ultimately, All-Entity's infinite reality is in us. This is why we are alive. Wouldn't it be nice to tap into this unlimited resource within? After all, we are one with All-Entity (**HP2** & **HP5**).

The ancient scriptures of Hinduism, the Vedas, call the innermost personal reality "Atman," and the ultimate reality of the universe "Brahman." A Hindu's goal is to experience Atman and Brahman as one. The final part of the Vedas is called The Upanishads and are dated

between the eighth and fourth centuries BC. A quote
from The Upanishads:

> The truth is that you are always united with the Lord. But
> you must know this. Nothing further is there to know.

The key to taking advantage of this unlimited resource is
to change your perspective. The way to do this is to
identify with All-Entity as your own innermost Self, the
essence of yourself. Then you will be in harmony with
your Self and with the rest of the world because All-
Entity is the total harmony of everything with everything.
It may sound idealistic and unrealistic, perhaps even a
little "too religious." But it is actually quite pragmatic,
enabling you to know reality as it is and to know "how the
cookie crumbles." Identification with All-Entity is the
path to enlightenment as taught by Jesus, Krishna,
Buddha, and other great mystics. They explained how to
awaken to the ultimate reality, which is deep within
ourselves and encompasses the whole universe.

All-Entity is the subject of religions. But here we will
avoid the doctrine and dogma of organized religion.
Modern society has learned to think rationally, and
Holistic Logic is rational. If by using Holistic Logic we
reach the same basic conclusion that world religions reach
through dogma, so much the better. Holistic Logic
describes the Truth in religion without having us become
sidetracked by misconceptions. However, Holistic Logic
is not the only correct way. Multi-dimensional reality
provides many ways to find the Truth, and each
individual's viewpoint differs at least somewhat from
those of others. However, if you are looking for a rational
approach to understanding the irrational, then this book
can help you. It can provide answers to questions such as:
Who are we, and who are you? Are you your ego, your

Self, your soul?   Or are you your innermost self, All-Entity?

You are all of these, and you can select the position you prefer. The ultimate Truth is that we are all One.

Chapter 8

Multiple Worlds

Astronomers estimate that the sun is only one of about 400 billion stars in our own galaxy, and that the whole universe consists of over 100 billion galaxies. Now quantum physics postulates boundless additional invisible realities "parallel" to ours, and Holistic Logic comes to the same conclusion. Quantum physicists believe that the multiple-world concept is the correct interpretation of scientific test results. Hugh Everett explored this concept mathematically in the 1950s, and it has been debated ever since. The prominent physicist Stephen Hawking says in his recent book, The Universe in a Nutshell,

> This idea that the universe has multiple histories may sound like science fiction, but it is now accepted as science fact.

When we illustrated Holon Principle **HP3** (The whole is invisible from the lower dimensional level of its parts), we observed that our imaginary 2D creatures were oblivious to other 2-D worlds in their crystal universe. That was because those planes were in the third dimension, beyond the 2Ds' perception. For a consciousness that is limited to two dimensions, only one of the surface planes exists. The rest of the crystal is invisible, including its other surface planes, even though they are just as real in 3-D. We also observed this principle when we discussed reincarnation (figures 2.5, 2.6).

Conceivably, the crystal could have a vast number of surface sections in addition to the one inhabited by the

2Ds. The 2Ds would not see any of them. Our crystal analogy is only a limited example. Theoretically, any 3-D space contains an infinite number of potential 2-D planes in all possible orientations. Similarly, a four-dimensional reality contains an infinite number of possible 3-D spaces that do not coincide with each other. We cannot picture this in our mind, but it makes sense logically and scientifically. We already discussed the four-dimensional spacetime of Einstein's Theory of Relativity.

You might try to imagine a geometric space with not only three, but with four or even more dimensions. However, this is a misleading approach. You come closer to the truth if you imagine reality as electro magnetic waves around you, with untold different frequencies over an unlimited frequency range. Imagine that someone is listening to a weather radio that is tuned to a particular frequency, the only frequency the radio receives. His environment is limited to weather news and nothing else. This may be exciting for someone interested in weather, and he may be satisfied with it if he knows nothing else. You are tuned into one reality in much the same way, just like the single minded weather-person. We are now beginning to realize that countless other realities exist, right here around us. We are simply not tuned into them. Instead of listening to weather news all our lives, we could choose exciting TV programs, if we only knew how to dial into them.

It is realistic to accept that we live among many other cultures in the same multi-dimensional environment without perceiving them. For instance, our own incarnations in different historical times live together with our present one in the same multi-dimensional reality without being able to see each other. Past, present, and future coexist in the present moment. This is possible because an unlimited number of 3-D worlds can coexist simultaneously in multi-dimensional reality without its inhabitants being aware of each other. The many 3-D worlds are all united in a multi-dimensional whole. They only seem to be separate worlds at their lower level (**HP4**). Your soul dwells in that multi-dimensional whole, while your different incarnations live simultaneously in different historical environments.

In Chapter 4 we visualized the nature of time as a path through a multi-dimensional landscape (figure 2.1). Multi-dimensional reality is like a landscape of events stretching far beyond our vision. We experience our own events, but an infinite number of other events occur unseen in all directions. They all have their own pasts and futures. This is an incredibly intricate network of individual destinies interweaving endlessly in a multi-dimensional fabric. All these strings of events form parallel worlds at their own level of reality. They are united into one whole at a higher dimensional level.

Another way to picture the multiple-world concept is as follows. Imagine taking a photo of a tree. We get a 2-D picture of the 3-D tree. This picture, being flat, is a 2-D reality. In Holistic Logic terms, this is one possible 2-D reality that is a part of and represents an aspect of the whole tree in 3-D reality (**HP4**), (figure 2.8).
We can go around the tree and take pictures from different angles. In other words, we create other 2-D realities of the same 3-D reality. We can take an unlimited number of different pictures. They are all real in 2-D, yet they represent the same 3-D reality, just different aspects of it. As we do this, we create one 2-D reality at a time, but the different aspects of the tree all exist simultaneously. All 3-D aspects are like potential 2-D worlds, but they are not realized as a 2-D reality until our camera "pays attention" like a 2-D consciousness. This

is how we create our 3-D world from multi-dimensional reality.

Figure 2.8a. Creating multiple 2-D realities
from a 3-D tree.

1. *Front View*   2. *Bottom View*   3. *Top View*

Figure 2.8b.   Three different 2-D aspects of a tree.

Transposing this 3-D example to higher dimensions, we can say that any multi-dimensional entity has unlimited diverse 3-D aspects, depending upon which viewpoint we take. **Every time we look at a multi-dimensional entity, we see only one 3-D aspect of it.** By looking at it, we make that particular aspect real in our consciousness. When we look at the tree, we really look at its multi-dimensional reality, but we only see three of its dimensions, because this is all our consciousness perceives. **Thus, we "create" a 3-D reality that would not be there without our consciousness.** If we do not look, there is only the multi-dimensional reality without someone limiting it to 3-D. This is similar to looking through a filter that eliminates all dimensions except our own three. All the dimensions are always there, right in front of your eyes, but your eyes are "multi-dimensionally blind," like being colorblind. A colorblind person may see only green, so he "creates" a green image and ignores the other colors. Another may see only red, and "creates" a different reality.

We can perceive the multi-dimensional tree from countless different viewpoints. Therefore we could potentially see countless different 3-D aspects of it. For each one we would "create" a different 3-D reality in our consciousness, while the multi-dimensional tree is always the same. We create the 3-D reality through our consciousness, because that is the only place where 3-D reality exists, in the human mind. The actual reality has countless more dimensions, as we have learned. Therefore, every tree, *every thing* in our world, is one of countless possible aspects of the real multi-dimensional thing-in-itself. Our viewpoint determines what we see of it. The physicist John Gribbin writes: "nothing is real unless we look at it, and it ceases to be real as soon as we stop looking." Physicists came to this conclusion when they had no other possible explanation for certain quantum phenomena. Events in 3-D reality occur only if a consciousness observes them. Otherwise, they do not appear in our world. Thus we create our experience in the physical reality.

As early as the 1700's the Irish philosopher and clergyman George Berkeley said that physical objects do not exist unless a mind perceives them. He thought this was so obvious that he could not understand why others disagreed. Berkeley must have sensed multi-dimensional reality. Your state of consciousness determines how you perceive reality. You are accustomed to thinking that there is an "objective" world out there and that all you need to do is to look at it "objectively" to see how it really is. **Now it turns out that your own consciousness determines what you see. This is a major challenge for scientists. Science is built on the belief that physical reality is independent of the mind. This assumption must now be revised.**

Your senses experience the particular multi-dimensional "channel" that you are tuned into; all other multi-dimensional aspects may be physical in other 3-D worlds, but not in yours. Each person creates his/her own experience by focusing on one of multi-dimensional reality's infinite probabilities. We find it difficult to accept the immensity of multiple worlds beyond ours only because we think of them as separate worlds. In reality, they are only different aspects of one single whole. Nothing is separate in nonlocal multi-dimensional reality, all is one, everything is All-Entity. Common sense cannot cope with the vastness of All-Entity, but the consoling thought is that your psyche can. It can deal with It because immanently your psyche is identical with All-Entity. Think of an individual in a great nation. As a single person, you could feel hopelessly insignificant, given the total population of the country. Yet, with the spirit of patriotism, it is uplifting to be part of that great country. You can adopt a similar attitude towards the universe and feel very good about it, knowing that it is in your heart and that it sustains you. All you have to do is to change your point of view – it is all in your mind.

Please note that no three-dimensional analogy describes all multi-dimensional principles simultaneously. The tree analogy is useful for picturing how we create our own reality from the untold probabilities of multi-dimensional reality, however it does not correctly portray how the whole and its parts are one (**HP6**), and how a part's change goes with a corresponding change in the whole (**HP10**). No analogy can portray more dimensions than it has itself.

* * *

The concept of multi-dimensional reality may sound esoteric. You may wonder what practical use it has. However, remember that the concept of atoms appeared to have no practical use for millennia, but who would doubt its profound impact on our lives. Understanding the laws of natural sciences, as physics, chemistry, and biology, has created our modern technology. Now our civilization faces a major crisis because it has not evolved spiritually. It is critical for humankind to understand the laws that govern mental, psychological, psychic, and spiritual phenomena. These laws are actually closer to your heart than physical events because they are immanent in you - and you yearn to understand them. Multi-dimensional reality has laws too, and they are more significant than the laws of physics (**HP5**, the reality of the whole is more significant than that of its parts).

Part 3

ENTERING

MULTI-DIMENSIONAL

REALITY

Chapter 9

Multi-Dimensional Communication

Communication with the greater reality beyond our physical world occurs all the time. This should not surprise you, because multi-dimensional reality and our reality are one. They are simply viewed from different perspectives. All material objects and events in our visible world represent aspects of the multi-dimensional reality. The different aspects of the whole appear as separate parts, when viewed from the lower dimensional level of the parts (**HP4**). And the whole is immanent in us as well as in the objects around us (**HP7**). Since the objects and events share the same whole that is in our psyche, they may even give us clues about our psychic climate, individually and collectively. We will discuss this subject in more detail later.

A few words about our terminology are now appropriate. We have arrived at the concept of multiple dimensions beyond our 3-D environment by using rational arguments that are supported by modern scientific insights. Our approach was to look at reality and try to make sense of our observations. We noticed that the most pervasive characteristic of reality is that everything is organized into wholes and their parts. Using the crystal analogy and other examples, we concluded that any whole has more dimensions than its parts. We also concluded that a part can't perceive its respective whole. Since we humans are parts within the universe, it follows logically that we cannot perceive the whole to which we belong. It also follows that this whole has more dimensions than our

3-D perception. In other words, the whole of which we are parts is multi-dimensional. All this is quite rational.

We can even make rational statements about the nature of multi-dimensional reality. For instance, that it is full of intelligent life which is more significant than that which we perceive at our own level (**HP5**). This is true because we, as parts, are alive, and, as such, we represent aspects of the multi-dimensional whole (**HP4**). Thus life is an aspect of that whole. And to be logically consistent, we assume that an ultimate whole exists for the entire universe. We called it All-Entity. Again, this is a rational assumption that emerges naturally from our logical process.

Now, it is quite obvious that these rational conclusions mirror what we call spirituality. The big difference is, however, that the spiritual is considered irrational, beyond human rationality. Spiritual concepts are a matter of faith without a scientifically supported rational framework. This eliminates any logical restriction and allows us free reign to hold beliefs that may not correspond to reality. We already encountered this difference when we compared the terms All-Entity and God. **This book presents a logic system that unites scientific and spiritual understanding, however this system does not support certain existing beliefs about spiritual reality.** In this sense, the term 'spirituality' is used here for the true reality that is beyond our perception. Religions express opinions about this spiritual reality, as mentioned earlier, and so does Holistic Logic. However, Holistic Logic is supported by scientific understanding, religion is not. It turns out that Holistic Logic comes to conclusions that are similar to some religious concepts. Also, Holistic Logic provides rational explanations for phenomena that were formerly considered irrational. One of these is communication with the spirit world.

PERSONAL COMMUNICATION

Spiritual reality is inside you, so it should be easily accessible. If you do not perceive this, it is because your mind is not open to multi-dimensional reality. You experience only what the dimensions of your mindset can encompass. The first precondition for spiritual perception is that you must shed any prejudice that you may have against it. To open communication with the multi-dimensional/spiritual reality within, you must first accept that it exists. You must hold the belief that you can communicate with your inner Self before you can do this successfully. You can learn to recognize messages that come from within. They come as thoughts, feelings, images, or words that surface in your mind, usually spontaneously. Reserve a daily quiet time for yourself. Relax and try to suspend your thinking. When your mind is reasonably still, pose a specific question. Address this question to your inner Self, your soul, or All-Entity, whichever feels comfortable to you. Without being anxious, wait for an answer. The answer will come, but not necessarily immediately. Sometimes you'll receive a message in unexpected ways, perhaps during the day in the middle of some routine activity, or even during a normal conversation that may impress you as being particularly meaningful. While reading a newspaper, you may unexpectedly find a passage that reads as if it was written just for you. Everyone receives such messages, but most people ignore them. Your inner psyche is always alert. It is aware of what is happening in multi-dimensional reality.

You may want to experiment with asking your question before you fall asleep, when your mind is calm and unoccupied. When you wake up in the morning, you may know the answer. I have done this several times in the course of writing this book when I encountered an impasse about how to treat a difficult subject. The answers appear to be obvious the next morning. We are so locked into our present viewpoint that we do not recognize the obvious answer. From a multi-dimensional perspective, all the answers to our perceived problems already exist. For every minus, there is a plus, for every down, there is an up, and for every bad, there is a good because multi-dimensionality is whole. Multi-dimensional reality provides a birds-eye view of physical reality.

Be careful not to let your ego interfere with your attempt to communicate with higher dimensions. I have met individuals who were in the habit of reading meanings into every little occurrence. It is important to recognize the source of such information. The ego can be like a child that interrupts an adult conversation just to get attention. Remember that your ego is that limited aspect of yourself with which you identify while physically alive. In other words, your ego is exactly that part of you that prevents you from perceiving multi-dimensional reality. If it were not for the ego's fewer dimensions, you would always be aware of multi-dimensionality. Strive to be relaxed and nonchalant. Anxiety disturbs communication with your inner Self. If you are too eager to find a solution to a problem, you may be so focused on the problem that your mind is not free to receive the solution. We will discuss this more in Chapter 10. A valid message from multi-dimensional reality comes spontaneously, with a good feeling. If it does not, it is best to ignore it.

Dreams are great communication links with multi-dimensional reality. They display multi-dimensional activity in a symbolic way. Individuals and situations that appear in a dream can have specific symbolic meanings. The emotional content of a dream is important for interpretation. Dream books cannot provide an explanation when the symbolism is related to personal characteristics or events known only to the dreamer. It is helpful to write your dreams down right after awakening, before your memory fades. Later you can take time to explore their meaning. Dreams can convey important messages about personal situations. For instance, an old enemy may appear in your dream. Ask yourself, what attitude does this person represent? How would you characterize him? What does he symbolize in your life? And could he perhaps represent one of your own traits that you have not yet acknowledged? Specific individuals in dreams can represent your own characteristics. A conflict with a dream personality could well mirror a conflict within yourself, or perhaps a challenge that you have unconsciously chosen and need to face. A nightmare can be like shock therapy chosen by your higher Self to make you face a certain issue. Our dreams are symbolic for our activities and situations in multi-dimensional reality. Try to sense the psychological significance of the story in the dream. We are quite active and productive while we are sleeping. Not all dreams can be understood, however, because they may reflect remote regions of the psyche.

CHANNELING OVERVIEW

In addition to our own inner communication with multi-dimensional reality, individuals with well-developed psychic abilities relate messages from multi-dimensional sources for our benefit. These individuals were once called mediums and are now referred to as channelers.

Holistic Logic supports the possibility of channeled information from the multi-dimensional domain. Remember that the whole and its parts are one and that you carry the multi-dimensional whole within yourself. Also, no divisions and separations exist in multi-dimensional reality (**HP9**). This means that all events and ideas in multi-dimensional reality are available anywhere, to anyone. It's simply a matter of tuning into this information, like a radio receiver. The degree to which you can access more dimensions than those of your ego depends on your psychic makeup. This is equivalent to owning a short wave radio receiver in addition to an AM and FM receiver. You have the potential of opening your mind to other dimensions in addition to your customary daytime consciousness, because your daytime consciousness is an integral part of your multi-dimensional consciousness, according to Holistic Logic.

Do multi-dimensional entities exist who are willing to channel information? Please remember again that we think of entities only because of our lower dimensional point of view that divides reality into separate entities (**HP4**). In reality, there are no separate entities, only different aspects of one whole. You are one such aspect. Communication between all aspects of the whole is a vital characteristic of life, it is the essence of wholeness.

If you have read this far, you probably accept that multi-dimensional reality exists. It teems with intelligent life. Multi-dimensional consciousness is more intelligent than ours, because it encompasses more dimensions. As our communication technology is based on physical laws, multi-dimensional communication uses multi-dimensional laws, such as telepathy. To communicate with us, some multi-dimensional entities choose to speak or write through a psychic who devotes her life to this service. As with everything else, there are good channelers and not so good channelers. You can tell them apart by the quality of their messages.

Jon Klimo's book, *"Channeling, Investigations on Receiving Information from Paranormal Sources"* (1998) is a substantial work with numerous examples. The author is a senior faculty member of the Rosebridge Graduate School of Integrative Psychology in Concord, California, where he directs the doctoral program in parapsychology. In his introduction, Jon Klimo explains that channeling has been practiced throughout human history and that it is an important facet of human nature. All great spiritual belief systems appear to be based on channeled information, according to Klimo.

Klimo's book covers all aspects of communication with multi-dimensional entities. Many examples are cited, such as deceased relatives proving their identity through messages with unique personal details that their survivors recognize. The channeling sources range from departed individuals through spiritual teachers, up to the collective unconscious (Humankind-Entity), Christ, and God. In reviewing the history of channeling, Klimo describes how shamans received guidance and healing power from the spirit world for their flocks. The ancient civilizations of Egypt and China practiced spirit communication through people in trance, and the Bible is full of reports of prophets, such as Moses, David, and Solomon, who had verbal contact with Yahweh. Socrates said that he had communicated with a "semi-divine" being, and the ancient Greeks consulted the oracle of Delphi for divine guidance. In Europe, Joan of Arc, Nostradamus, Emanuel Swedenburg, and many others demonstrated psychic communication.

During the past three centuries, prevailing scientific belief suppressed activities such as these. Then, in 1848, the Fox sisters, two farmer's daughters from New York State, demonstrated a stunning capability to communicate with deceased individuals. This started the Spiritualism movement with mediums relating messages from multi-dimensional realms. Numerous scientific tests were performed which should have proven the validity of spirit communication. Even President Lincoln used the services of a medium. However, science was not yet ready to accept spiritual reality, and Spiritualism went underground. Klimo's book discusses the various channeling methods such as full trance, conscious channeling, and automatic writing, where the multi-dimensional source directs the channeler's hand. Some multi-dimensional sources explain their communication technology in general terms. Jon Klimo suggests possible scientific explanations and describes how you can develop your own channeling capability. The amount of detailed and specific material contained in Jon Klimo's book, supported by a wealth of references, is impressive. It provides a convincing argument that intelligent communication with the spirit world exists. As Dr. Zammit said of his research into the afterlife, any one of the countless examples may be questionable, but the totality of evidence is overwhelming.

JANE ROBERTS

Some of my favorite channeled literature is that of Jane Roberts (1929-1984). She was an excellent psychic who, with her husband Robert Butts' dedicated help, created a number of books dictated by Seth, a personality who no longer lives in our physical reality. Seth describes the multi-dimensional reality where he resides as well as possible using our limited language. His explanations mirror Holistic Logic so much that I lost previous doubts about the viability of channeled communication. Seth's explanations of multi-dimensional reality reflect my own understanding, and the preceding chapters would not have been as detailed without my exposure to the Seth material. His books clearly project a superior intelligence. His knowledge is far reaching, his insight into the psyche is most impressive, and his descriptions of multi-dimensional reality portray first-hand experience. His narrative is spiced with a "down-to-Earth" humor that suggests a wealth of practical life experience. A personality of his caliber does not need to resort to deception to sell his books. Jane Roberts' Seth books include: *The Seth Material* (1970), *Seth Speaks* (1972), *The Nature Of Personal Reality* (1974), *The "Unknown" Reality* (2 Volumes1977/79), *The Nature Of The Psyche* (1979), and *The Individual And The* Nature of Mass Events (1981).

An introductory note in *The Seth Material* states that Jane Roberts had never before considered herself a psychic and that she had not even believed in life after death. Yet, her communication with the Seth-entity became a channeling milestone. In her introduction to *Seth Speaks*, Roberts describes her first channeling experience which occurred in 1963. She was a writer, and as she sat writing poetry, she suddenly felt her consciousness leave her body. Her mind was exposed to a host of ideas totally new and astounding to her. When she regained her normal state of consciousness, she found that she had written down explanations of these ideas. This was a new and unexpected experience for Jane Roberts, and it motivated her to investigate psychic activity and to write a book about it. She and her husband experimented with a Ouija board. This advanced the psychic connection with Seth and eventually enabled her to speak his words aloud while in trance.

Seth describes how All That Is (God) represents the reality from which everything comes, and that All

That Is transcends all dimensions of reality and consciousness, while still being intimately united with each part. Consciousness is within everything, even within inanimate matter. Seth explains that reincarnations are simultaneous, parallel existences in timeless multidimensional reality. Of course we think of them as past or future events. He repeatedly states that each one of us creates our own physical reality, and as a society, we all create "the glories and the terrors" that exist in our earthly experience. Seth also says that events can be changed both before and after they occur in our three-dimensional environment, because time does not exist in true, multidimensional reality.

This very brief, albeit incomplete, synopsis shows why Seth, through Jane Roberts, is one of my favorite authors. His explanations agree perfectly with what I had experienced more than half a century ago. I understood then that past, present, and future are simultaneous, and that our soul's incarnations exist simultaneously in a multi-dimensional environment beyond time. But Seth describes this much more extensively and in vivid detail. He is speaking from his "home territory."

COMMUNICATION WITH GOD AND JESUS.

Before we continue, we should make some comments about channelings from God and Jesus. Jon Klimo mentioned such communications in his book, and the channelers mentioned below claim God or Jesus as their sources. You may ask, as my daughter Carol did: "If All-Entity is so multi-dimensional and if we should not consider It in human terms, then how is it possible for "God" to sit down and have a chat? It's a big leap from hearing channeled information from a "higher entity" to hearing it from God."

This question goes to the crux of Holistic Logic. How can a vast, undifferentiated multi-dimensional whole focus its attention on one small individual part? According to Holistic Logic, this is possible because the multiple dimensions of the whole allow for a myriad of different aspects of that whole. Each person is an aspect of God.   Each person is one with God. The only difference is that God and persons are perceived from different dimensional levels (**HP2**). Because God and an individual are one, there is nothing insignificant about an individual!   We can't imagine the enormity of this, because we lack the dimensional scope. We know that we can wiggle our little finger, but we cannot imagine that God would communicate with an individual. The difference is only one of scale, not one of principle.

I don't know whether it was God or Jesus who spoke though the channelers, but I believe that it is possible based on Holistic Logic.   You can also imagine successive communication stages, if a single step between God and us seems too large.   If you can accept that channeling is possible between a multi-dimensional entity and you, then it should be possible for this entity to receive channeled information from an even higher level, and so forth. The entity who speaks through a channeler to us could well speak in the name of God or Jesus if the message comes originally from God or Jesus. Anyway, it makes no difference because all stages of the communication are one with God.

Be this as it may, our only choice is to decide whether a message reveals truth or not, regardless of where it comes from.   I referred to the channeled messages here

because they agree with Holistic Logic, and I don't
attempt to substantiate their original source. This
situation is no different from any other information we
receive. We must decide for ourselves whether we want
to accept it or not. I believe that the discussed channeled
information is true, and that the quality of the information
is compatible with what God or Jesus might say to us, but
I do not know whether They said it.

HELEN COHN SCHUCMAN

In 1975, Helen Cohn Schucman published *A Course in
Miracles.* The work is over 1200 pages long and was in
the making for seven years. Many believe the source of
the book to be Jesus Christ. The book's contents justify
this assumption. Mrs. Schucman says of herself,
"Psychologist, educator, conservative in theory and
atheistic in belief, I was working in a prestigious and
highly academic setting." Eventually she started
receiving clearly symbolic dreams and strange images,
and she decided to record them. Helen Schucman reports
that, with time, she had grown more accustomed to the
unexpected, yet she was still very surprised when she
found herself writing inadvertently, 'This is a course in
miracles.' That was Mrs. Schucman's first experience of
what she calls "the Voice," an inner sensation that she
recorded in a shorthand notebook. The *Course* consists of
three major parts: Text, Workbook for Students, and
Manual for Teachers.

Its Preface states, that a universal theology is
impossible, but that experience of universal Oneness is
ultimately not only possible but necessary. The book is
written in Christian terminology, however it states that the
spiritual Truth can be expressed in different forms that

may appear contradictory but lead to the same experience of God. Disregarding its traditional religious terminology, *The Course of Miracles* agrees with Holistic Logic.

TOM CARPENTER

Tom Carpenter and his wife Linda published their channeled book, *Dialogue on Awakening, Communication with Jesus* in 1992. It explains in a heartwarming, loving way how you can abandon your false concept of separation from God. The book encourages you to "change your mind", to dismiss the thought of separation, and that this will automatically lead you "home again." According to Carpenter's writings, the human mind has never existed apart from the mind of God, and that total acceptance of this fact is all that is necessary to lead you back to experience your existing union with God.

Carpenter's book emphasizes also that we are one with Jesus, that we are the same, and that the only difference between him and us is that he is aware of this, and we are not. He asks us not to elevate him to a level that seems unattainable for us because this does not agree with true reality.

NEALE DONALD WALSCH

Neale D. Walsch published his first book, *Conversations with God, an uncommon dialogue,* in 1995. He describes how he was introduced to channeling when, out of desperation, he wrote a passionate letter to God. To Walsch's great surprise, he received an answer that he recorded immediately. This developed into a conversation that he recorded and published in several books. The tone of this conversation is surprisingly down-to-earth. Walsch repeatedly doubted and questioned the nature of the source and the validity of the messages, yet he concluded that he could not have imagined better answers than the ones he received. *Conversations with God* is a bestseller trilogy. The first book deals mainly with our personal lives, how they are part of the overall divine process and how we can live up to our challenges. Book two paints a picture of humanity's present situation, aimed at motivating us to avoid global calamity by changing course. The third book elaborates on the first two books, explaining the cosmic process, and describing highly evolved cultures that live throughout the universe.

As Walsch's conversation with God progresses, it becomes increasingly jovial, more like a chat between good friends. This trend continues through the subsequent books, *Friendship with God* (1999) and *Communion with God* (2000). There appears to be a deliberate attempt to remove the idea of separation from God and this attempt is largely successful. Corresponding to the previously mentioned books, Neale Walsch states that you create your reality. Life can only appear to you in accordance with your thoughts. This is how creation works.

Neale Walsch and his wife Nancy are now very actively spreading the message of his books around the world.

Chapter 10

Creating Your Own Reality

PSYCHIC DYNAMICS

Your changing thoughts and emotions change your mind and, through it, your Self, and your soul, because a change in a part corresponds to a change in the whole (**HP8**). In turn, the soul's change affects all its other incarnations (**HP10**). These incarnations, seemingly situated in the past and future, appear remote to us, but the timeless soul is always united with its incarnations and influences them in the present. Sometimes our moods may change for no apparent reason. We may be depressed, or we may be on top of the world. These feelings may originate in the subtle communication that exists between all the incarnations of the soul. In a multi-dimensional whole, a change of any part affects all other parts (**HP10**).

Similarly, your own experiences may affect your co-incarnations. We underestimate the power of our thoughts, they reverberate through the invisible reality with effects we do not suspect. A continuous give-and-take occurs between the soul and its incarnations. This concept flies against your common sense, but your common sense is limited; it does not consider multi-dimensional reality, where past, present, and future coexist in timelessness. Once you change your thinking to act in accordance with actual reality, you can use the power that you did not know you had.

For instance, people believe that they are at the mercy of their past. "You cannot change the past" is a phrase you take for granted. But the past is present now in multi-dimensional reality. You can still change it. **We can change the effect of past events on our lives by changing their emotional content.** Usually it is the emotional content of events that we would like to change. Suppose you had a disagreement with a good friend that caused a breakup years ago. You may regret what happened and you wish you could make amends. To do so, give yourself some undisturbed quiet time and relax. Then picture the past event in your mind and fill it with love, unrestricted, openhearted love, with no strings attached. Don't think of the disagreeable part of the event, but think of a warm, mutual relationship. Forgive him or her, and forgive yourself. Fill the relationship with the most joyful emotion you can produce. Perhaps imagine how you are embracing each other. Mentally and emotionally, replace the old situation with the one you wish had happened. Bless your relationship. Think of nothing else as long as you can stay relaxed and alert, say for five to ten minutes. Then let go of it completely and consider it done. Do not think about it any more. Do not doubt the effect of your meditation. After having performed it a few times, you will feel that the relationship with your friend is okay now. The regrets and bad feelings are gone. The past has been changed.

This procedure works because the event still exists in multi-dimensional reality. By replacing your emotions with positive ones, you change that part of multi-dimensional reality. The same part of multi-dimensionality also exists in your friend's psyche, and it is immanent in her mind. She will begin to feel differently about your disagreement. Over time, she will be inclined to change her mind about what took place between the two of you. You do not control her mind, but you changed multi-dimensional reality and its effect on her.

Consider this event a holon. The event is the whole in multi-dimensional reality and the memories in the minds of both persons are its parts (figure 3.1). A change in one person's mind changes the whole, and this in turn changes the other person's mind immanently, according to Holon Principles 8 and 10. We call it mental telepathy and it works if you believe in it. Your belief in a positive outcome is part of the message that you place into multi-dimensional reality (M-D). This does not mean, however, that you can change someone's mind against their will. You can send out your message telepathically, but the other person has the right to control her own mind. If you try the example above, you will still end up with the satisfaction of having at least done your part.

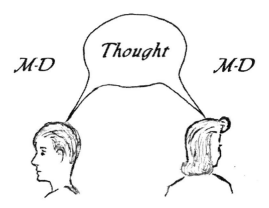

Figure. 3.1. Telepathy holon

The key is to believe without a doubt in the reality of your imagination. You literally create a thought pattern. We all have the power to do so. Thoughts are distinct objects in multi-dimensional reality as material things are objects

in physical reality. Jesus told us about the power of belief
two thousand years ago. Now we understand "the
mechanics" of this process. Those who believe that
physical reality is more fundamental than mental reality
may not accept this. For them it will not work, because
they will get what they believe.

You cannot mentally change physical evidence of past
events, such as documents, and you cannot reverse a bad
stock trade. But you can change the psychological
reaction, the mental and emotional interpretation of these
events, and this is what ultimately counts. Once you do
this, the physical aspects fade into the background and
they lose their significance. In a way, they disappear
from sight. So you see, you have changed the nature of
the physical events without altering their form. Let's take
the example of an unfortunate stock trade. Assume that
you bought Enron stocks just before their precipitous
nosedive. From the holistic, multidimensional viewpoint,
the only thing that is important is how this event affects
you emotionally. The dollars themselves have no reality
beyond the value and emotion that you attach to them.
Therefore you may choose between being emotionally
devastated by this loss, or you may think of it as a
challenge to use your power of positive thinking.

If you allow your thinking to be governed by
disappointment, then you will create that which you think
about. You will experience more disappointment. If,
however, you change your experience by replacing your
disappointment with the belief that you will be provided
for, no matter what happens, then you will attract this
reality. You will realize that you can make use of
unfortunate events in your life to practice shaping your
destiny through your beliefs. This approach is less fickle
than the stock market! The more vividly you can imagine
your desired future, the sooner you will experience what

you want. You may not even notice how smoothly your life is moving toward your heart's desire. You have changed your past event by changing the nature of its emotional significance.

Multi-dimensional reality is more significant than physical events in our 3-D reality because the reality of the whole has more significance than that of its parts (**HP5**). Thoughts and emotions are the stuff of multi-dimensional reality. They spawn and influence events in our physical world. Once you understand how your mental activity influences the multi-dimensional environment, and through it the physical world, you can use this knowledge to your advantage as well as to the advantage of others. This is the "technology" of the future, the new common sense of the third millennium. The foregoing example is only a small part of it. Your potential for future development is unlimited because each one of us immanently carries All-Entity's potential.

HOW YOU CREATE YOUR REALITY

We all create our own reality, individually and collectively, as a family, as a society, and as the human race. The problem is that we are usually not aware of this. Most people are not conscious of their mindset and how it selects their reality from untold multi-dimensional possibilities. They cannot see how their mindset shapes their future, how it resonates with corresponding hidden probable events, bringing these events to the fore. Jane Roberts describes this process eloquently in her book *The Nature of Personal Reality, A Seth Book.* Seth explains how you create your own reality and how you can create the reality you desire. His statement "You Make Your Own Reality" pervades the entire book. He cites two other fundamental truths: "The Self Is Not Limited" and "There Are No Boundaries or Separations of the Self." This agrees with Holistic Logic's view that All-Entity is the ultimate immanent whole of the Self (**HP7**), and that no divisions and separations exist in multi-dimensional reality (**HP9**).

Referring to the tree analogy of Chapter 8, you will recall that your mind selects one particular aspect from multi-dimensional reality's enormous reservoir of probable events. All are ready to be called into physical reality depending upon your mindset. Your mind selects a specific probability by paying attention to it, like a teacher who looks at one of her pupils to encourage an answer. The contents of your mind make up your mindset. We are not talking about fleeting, extraneous thoughts, but about ingrained thought patterns, such as beliefs about the world, about others, and about yourself. These patterns are embedded in your mind and you normally don't even pay attention to them, but they are so deeply seated in your psyche that they stand out in multi-dimensional reality. There they "automatically" resonate with corresponding potential events. This is a multi-dimensional law: **like attracts like** because like subjects form holons whose wholes unite them. If we nurture resentful thoughts, we draw resentment towards us. If we give love, we will receive love in return. We reap what we sow.

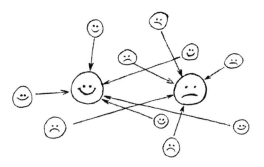

Figure 3.2.   Like attracts like.

No separation exists in multi-dimensional (M-D) reality. Therefore, thought patterns and corresponding events join easily. Usually we are not aware of this process. We do not notice that we could choose other equally valid events, but that our minds are not tuned into them. Thus we create our specific personal reality out of unlimited possibilities. When we are not aware of our mindsets, we are like blind people creating a painting. Most likely it will not turn out as well as we would like.

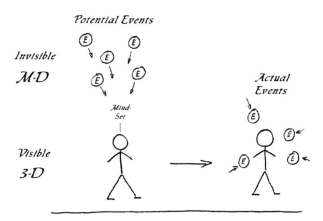

Figure 3.3. Creating your experiences

The good news is that you do not have to continue living that way, you need not limit your choices. You can learn to consciously choose the best opportunities available from the wealth of multi-dimensional possibilities. To do so requires that you become aware of the contents of your mind. When you are no longer on autopilot, but are conscious of what your mindset chooses, you can decide to alter the choice. By controlling your mindset, you can select what you like from multi-dimensional reality's unlimited probable events.

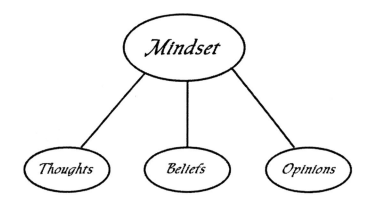

Figure 3.4. Mindset holon.

Your habitual thoughts and all your beliefs together form the whole of your mindset in a holon. You can't observe your mindset directly (The whole is invisible from the lower dimensional level of its parts, **HP3**), but you can recall your thoughts and beliefs one at a time (The different aspects of the whole appear as separate parts, when viewed from the lower dimensional level of the parts, **HP4**). Seth recommends the following procedure to create a mindset for the reality you want. It is a four-step process.

Step 1: Write down all your beliefs. A belief is simply an opinion about what is true or not. It may or may not have anything to do with religion. For instance, what is your opinion of yourself? Do you believe that you are inferior, equal, or superior to others? Do you believe that life is complicated or a joyful experience? Do you worry about the future or about what you should have done differently in the past? The more you write down, the more easily you'll remember other beliefs that dwell in your mind. This method applies not only to beliefs that may have an undesirable effect on your life. The object is to become conscious of all personal beliefs, positive and negative. You should not make this a labored effort, rather be relaxed but persistent. Hold any thoughts that arise to the surface of your mind. Also write down thoughts that you may consider objectionable. They could block access to other ideas that are perfectly legitimate and are waiting to be addressed.

Notice that some beliefs belong together, they are variations on a main theme. Try to formulate this underlying theme in one concise sentence. Seth calls such main themes "core beliefs." They are significant beliefs that spawn secondary sub-beliefs, like parts of a holon. For example, you may believe that you do not look good, are too fat, have no friends, are not intelligent enough, etc. The core belief in this case is that you are inferior to others. In other words you have low self-esteem. Self-deprecation is a false belief, because your true immanent nature is glamorous indeed, since you are an aspect of All-Entity.

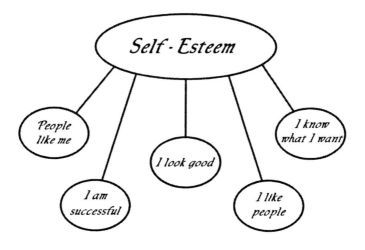

Figure 3.5.   Holon of core belief and sub-beliefs.

Identifying core beliefs is important.   If these beliefs
don't serve you and are then corrected, all their sub-
beliefs come tumbling down, freeing you in one fell
swoop from a host of limitations.   Make sure, however,
that you do not pursue a campaign of finding out "what is
wrong with you."   If you presume that something is
wrong with you, then you will create exactly that:
something wrong with you.   We create what we believe.
The more we search for problems, the more we will find
them.   I did this, and it wasn't much fun.   The correct
approach is to be relaxed, neutral and forgiving.   It works
like brainstorming.   First you create a list of beliefs
without judging them. After that you examine them.

Some beliefs may seem so self-evident that you do
not even think of them.   You consider them as obvious
truths and do not realize that they are only your beliefs
about truths. For instance, you may be habitually worried

about something going wrong, believing that this is just how life is. Yes, things will go wrong for you, so you will feel justified in your habit of worrying. However this is not because life is intrinsically worrisome, but because your belief creates those worrisome occasions. Most of them are probably harmless events that you consider worrisome because of your bias. It's a vicious cycle. Seth calls such beliefs "invisible beliefs." You might think that they are so deeply seated that you cannot reach them. Actually, these invisible beliefs are on the surface and so pervasive that you do not notice them. They are too obvious to register. It's like searching for your eyeglasses while you are wearing them.

In another case, you might take it for granted that people cannot be trusted. You will find countless episodes that substantiate your belief and you will ignore or not recognize those that demonstrate trustworthiness. Your distrust will be continually justified and reinforced. It never occurs to you that it is your belief that causes you to experience mistrust. You mistake your belief for truth, and this renders your belief invisible to you.

Step 2: Once you have developed your list of beliefs, examine each one to see whether it is still correct. Ask yourself: would I agree with someone who expressed such a belief? Usually, some beliefs will need to be corrected. Either they are outright incorrect, or more often, they do not apply to all circumstances. For instance, if you believe that it is always right to be nice to others, your belief will work quite well, except when you are physically or emotionally attacked. You may want to modify your belief for such situations. Many beliefs are carried over from childhood. You accepted them because you had to. Now, as a mature person, you must make up your own mind. Some people may be surprised at how many conflicting ideas they carry with them, causing unnecessarily suffering. **Our feelings and emotions are products of our beliefs, and we control them through the beliefs we choose.**

Step 3: After having identified the false beliefs, you are now able to correct them as appropriate, one by one. This takes some thought, but it is well worth the effort. It's helpful to talk about this with a trusted friend. Write down the new, corrected belief in one single, concise sentence, as clearly as possible, without ambiguity. This statement must be positive. For instance, you should say, "I am perfectly healthy" instead of, "I am not sick any more."   Another important point to remember is to speak in the present tense. Do not say, "I will be healthy," instead say, "I **am** healthy." Only the present is real. If you say, "I will be healthy," you imply that you are not healthy now and that you do not believe that you are healthy. This belief then creates your reality. The driving thought behind your statement is what counts. This example given to promote health is effective only if you first remove any beliefs, opinions or attitudes that may upset your mental and spiritual harmony. In other words, eliminate the beliefs that caused the illness to begin with, such as self-recrimination, resentment, or conflicting goals.

Step 4: After you are satisfied with your new belief statement, implant it in your mind so that it becomes second nature. Just settling on a new belief statement is not enough. It must be firmly imbedded in the psyche to wipe out the old belief. Only then will you live by the new belief intuitively. Only then has your mindset changed enough to attract the new reality. This is similar to learning a poem that you remember for the rest of your life. Seth describes how to do this with autosuggestion. Reserve a quiet period every day, preferably in the morning, when your mind is rested and clear. During this time, focus on your new belief and repeat your new statement for five to ten minutes, aloud if possible. Picture yourself acting according to your new belief.

Eventually you will sense that "you got it," and you can proceed in assimilating   another revised belief. Experiment with how many of these autosuggestions you can handle comfortably in one session.   With time, you will act according to the new belief, first by reminding yourself, later intuitively.   You have changed your mindset by holding different beliefs.   As a result, you attract events that correspond to your intentions.   They will fall into place naturally.

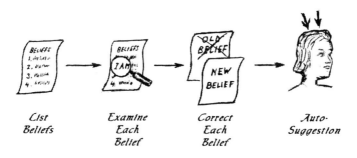

| List Beliefs | Examine Each Belief | Correct Each Belief | Auto- Suggestion |

Figure 3.6, Mindset correction process

When I was in my late teens and early twenties I prided myself on my ability to live with minimum means. The post-war famine and chaos in Germany had taught me how to survive on a shoestring and I believed in the virtue of needing very little. The Spartans of ancient Greece were my role models. I saw something heroic in this concept, and it has served me well through various challenges. I developed a distaste for material wealth. This was a strong belief, and as with any belief, I experienced the result. I did not understand this at the time and I made no conscious decision to change this belief before I married. Consequently, my young family had to face a period of severe dearth. This unpleasant experience changed my attitude about money, but even after we were more prosperous, I still had this nagging feeling that we should not buy what was not absolutely necessary, and we should not spend money just for enjoyment.

It was not until I read Seth's explanation of the nature of beliefs that I realized the true cause of our exaggerated frugality. We abandoned our belief in scarcity and replaced it with a belief in the abundance of the universe. Now, my wife, Erika, and I do not even think about lack, and we enjoy our retirement with travel, leisure, and with living true to our beliefs. Sure, we watch the stock market and prefer it to go up. But it is not an issue with us. We just know that there will always be enough.

Within a couple of decades we had replaced many of our beliefs. Usually it was not a matter of eradicating an old belief, but modifying it by defining exactly where it applied and where it didn't, for example, the belief that "you must do your duty." Having grown up in the Prussian part of Germany, we absorbed this thinking with our mothers' milk. However, I later modified my belief. I now let love play a much larger role if there is a conflict between obligations and demands. The belief to do your duty, strictly applied, can lead to big trouble. As a young soldier, I had to swear absolute devotion and obedience to Adolf Hitler. I accepted this as a political reality in my life that could not be avoided. Any resistance to it was suicidal. Towards the war's end, this oath meant fighting "to the last drop of blood," as we were often told, regardless of how many civilian casualties it caused. Fortunately, I did not encounter this situation. Clearly, a higher duty to humankind superceded the given oath, but it required a conscious belief-adjustment, which some people could not make in the chaos. The general in command of the war zone in our area eventually made the decision to lay down all weapons. Subsequently he shot himself. His honor required it.

The time and effort you devote to revise and correct your mindset pays off handsomely. It removes the clutter in your mind and clarifies your thinking. You'll enjoy the feeling of conscious living and the certainty of your values. Eventually you will notice every thought and every word that disagrees with your beliefs, and you'll correct them on the spot. Be persistent but gentle with yourself. When you practice love and forgiveness, include yourself. In fact, you cannot truly love anyone unless you love yourself. By this I mean your true Self, not the misconception of yourself that is your ego.

As you routinely observe physical hygiene for your body, so should you practice routine hygiene for your mind. No thought exists in a vacuum; every thought has an effect. Everything is interconnected. Even idle thoughts reverberate through multi-dimensional reality. The fact that we do not see them does not mean that this does not occur. The TV programs, literature, and music you let your children take in, do make a difference.

You are learning to apply multi-dimensional laws. These laws seem hidden from you, just as the laws of physics once were. Yet you can also understand the multi-dimensional laws and use them to your advantage. Your understanding of multi-dimensional laws will produce a new common sense that improves your life. Imagine having the power to create the future you want, materially and emotionally, both individually and as a society. This is a realistic goal and we can do this if enough people open their minds to multi-dimensional reality, a reality we already carry in our hearts.

You are not limited to the self that you think you are. Your ego-consciousness is only a small part of your real Self. Your total "I am" is unlimited. As long as you believe that you are only the self that you are experiencing now, you keep on re-creating that same self with its limitations. However, you can do much better than that, now that you understand the system. Everyone can be as great a person as he can imagine, and we can all create a truly advanced society. Our psyches have unlimited dimensions. Only our limited beliefs prevent us from using them. Think of every eliminated false belief as a new dimension gained. As we proceed, we will eliminate ever more powerful false core beliefs. The most important false core belief is that we are separated from All-Entity.

Jane Roberts' Seth books include many more practical exercises using multi-dimensional laws to create the life you want. An increasing number of books are now on the market that describe similar techniques, for instance Shakti Gawain's bestseller *Creative Visualization*. You understand through Holistic Logic that a vivid imagination and visualization changes your mindset and that this in turn attracts and creates your visualized situation to your reality (figure 3.3). It is important to deeply relax during this exercise and to let go of any interfering thoughts. The deep relaxation opens up the multi-dimensional realm of your psyche, and eliminating interfering thoughts enhances the influence of your visualization on your mindset. Shakti Gawain's *Creative*

Visualization book contains many specific practical examples. It is a good "how-to" book. Just remember that such "positive thinking" techniques work only if you do not hold contradictory beliefs. If you are unsatisfied with your progress or you continue to doubt the desired outcome, then try to identify any lingering conflicting beliefs using the mindset correction process described above (figure 3.6).

Try to understand the multi-dimensional "mechanism" of these visualization exercises in order to avoid disappointments. You will call into reality whatever is in your mind during the exercise. Therefore, make sure that you are aware of what is in your mind. If you perform a visualization to be rich because you worry about money, then your worry sets the tone, and you will create more money worries. During the exercise, you should make-believe that you are already wealthy, regardless of appearances. Two millennia ago, Jesus said, "I assure you, if you have faith and do not doubt, you can do things like this and much more." He was trying to teach us the facts of multi-dimensional reality.

It may be difficult not to think of a calamity when you are in the middle of it. If you are about to lose your job and can't let go of your anxiety during your visualization exercise, don't do it. If you are afraid during the exercise, you create what you fear, not what you want. Then you push two conflicting concepts simultaneously, the feared one and the desired one. This can become quite stressful. At least during the exercise, you should imagine the desired situation as if it already exists, with all the joy and carefree feeling that goes with success.

Creative visualization aimed at changing your reality works best when your mind is tuned into All-Entity because All-Entity already potentially contains all conceivable events, including the one you desire. You associate your mind with the most significant multi-dimensional level (**HP5**); This makes your reality change most effective. Prayer is very similar to a well performed visualization exercise. You may think that prayers seem to go unanswered too often. You may have prayed, "Oh God, get me out of this mess!" Note how all your attention was focused on the "mess," so this prayer may well have made matters worse. Actually, the desired solution already existed in multi-dimensional reality. For every aspect that appears in our 3-D world, an opposite aspect exists in multi-dimensional reality that could be pulled into your reality. It exists because everything is balanced in All-Entity, otherwise All-Entity would not be whole. Your prayers are answered before you pray, but it takes the proper mindset to "collect" the answer. The proper mindset is a total belief in the outcome.

Erika and I have had some experience along this line. At one time we had made a substantial real estate investment that went sour, and we did not know how to pay off a large mortgage. We prayed and we exercised creative visualization, but we did not notice that fear had motivated our meditations.

Then Erika suddenly received a very forceful message: "STOP IT!" She did not know where it had come from, but it had a profound emotional effect on her, and she couldn't have continued to meditate, even if she had wanted to. We discussed what had happened, and we understood that we were actually aggravating our situation with our fear-driven thoughts. We managed to clear our minds and to mentally identify with a positive outcome. The immediate effect was that we were calmer and more collected. Within a couple of weeks, we were able to sell the property at a reasonable price. The remaining loss was covered by insurance. Unfortunately, the insurance agent found out that we owned some stock, and he vowed not to pay the insurance until we had drained that reserve. Two weeks later we were pleasantly surprised to hear that he had been reassigned to another job. The new agent caused no further trouble. It could have been a lucky coincidence, but we were convinced that our concentration upon a positive outcome turned the tide in our favor.

In hindsight, we understood why we had gotten into this trouble to begin with. Our motivation for investing in real estate was not that we enjoyed it, or that we liked the challenge, but we were concerned that we might not have been able to afford good college educations for our three children. It was our belief in scarcity that motivated us, and that is what we got: scarcity. Fortunately, we learned our lesson.

Instead of using prayer to request help, you may prefer the view that multi-dimensional reality has unlimited possibilities, and that your own determination draws certain experiences to you. Therefore, if you have clear goals and believe in yourself, you can accomplish whatever you want. Note that both explanations are the same, as seen from different viewpoints, because All-Entity and the real You are one.

Not long ago I was having a problem with nagging heartburn in connection with what doctors call esophageal reflux syndrome. Even though I had followed the prescribed remedies, which included expensive medication, I had to get up at night and sit for hours to get relief. Eventually I remembered and practiced creative visualization. There is no proof that practicing it solved my problem, but I am now off medication and I can sleep soundly once again.

We had a much more dramatic experience that, for us, demonstrated the power of prayer. When our second daughter, Karen, was six years old, she started making odd mistakes in arithmetic, adding number columns incorrectly. Then she began to run into trees during play. We found out that she had developed double vision, and a medical examination concluded that she had a brain tumor. While she was in the hospital, we contacted a psychic in New York who confirmed this diagnosis and recommended that we pray for Karen's help. We did so with support from all our friends. When we saw Karen in her hospital bed the next morning, she greeted us happily and said that we could take her home. She claimed that she had awakened during the night and could see everything clearly. Karen was totally convinced that she was healthy. After some observation time and further examinations, her doctors concluded that she had had a "spontaneous remission" and that the tumor was gone. Every parent will understand our tremendous relief.

MY OWN APPROACH

I wish I had had Seth's books when, as a young man, I decided to implement my newly discovered truth after the enlightening experience I described in the Introduction. I was not sure where to start. A number of Hermann Hesse's books led me to Eastern philosophies that appeared to be more relevant than the Christianity to which I had been previously exposed. I read the Bhagavad Gita, a Hindu scripture that agreed with my own basic concept, but it did not tell me clearly just how to proceed. I also found a faction of the Theosophical Society within cycling distance and read parts of Madame Blavatzky's Secret Doctrine, which seemed too obscure for me.

Eventually I decided to focus on clearing myself of undesirable attitudes, since this seemed to be the prerequisite to experiencing permanent oneness with All-Entity. I sensed that our collective lifestyle was obviously flawed, judging by the devastation all around me. I did not want to escape reality. Rather, I had sensed the true reality, and it was a lot more desirable for everyone. If I didn't go after it, how could I expect anyone else to do so?

So I started my self-examination and improvement effort. I attacked my new task vigorously. After all, I had succeeded many times before through determined struggle. There was plenty to do, and the more I looked for flaws, the more I found. First, it was obvious that I was too self-centered. An older fellow in the military had taught me that all moral guidelines were just a thin veneer to cover up reality. You had to do for yourself whatever you could get away with. And this had worked for me. Thanks to his advice I had come unscathed through the war's turbulent end. I had also learned from experience that I was strongest when I relied upon myself. I had learned to fight for my survival in the previous years and had become street-smart. I knew how to maneuver through dangerous situations. Together with a comrade, I had walked some 300 miles through enemy-occupied territory where all travel was prohibited, and it took all my wits to escape capture. I had a couple of narrow escapes.

After Germany's capitulation, I traveled alone through West Germany trying to reach Berlin, but could not cross the Elbe River. The Russians on the other side shot anybody who tried. Eventually I crossed the "green border" farther south which separated the zones that were occupied by the Western Allies from the Soviet zone.[1] I crept through thick underbrush, knowing perfectly well that this could cost my life. But I was used to that by then. We joked about "air pollution" and "too much iron

[1] The Soviet Union was still considered an ally at that time.

content," when we spoke of the bullets and shells aimed at us.

But all this was in the past. I knew that I had to change my attitude. I was cocky. I was so sure of myself that I cared little about others. I must have stepped on some toes in those days without realizing it. But whenever I did realize it, I became distraught and worried about my insensitivity. Then I wondered, how much I actually understood other people's feelings. I remember an episode when a friend of mine stopped seeing a girl. She had obviously been in love with him, and I just did not understand how she could not get over the separation. I realized that I was unfamiliar with a whole dimension of life. My upbringing in military service had not trained me for this. Even prior to that, something must have been missing in my family, or I must have forgotten it. I had considered emotions as something that interfered with clear thinking, so I disregarded them whenever I needed to make a clear decision, and this had worked well to get me through life.

But now I started to doubt myself. Was I missing something by avoiding my emotions? Just about then I started to run into problems with my sweetheart, whom I had met at Blaupunkt Werke. I admired her for her clear face, her poise, and her natural self-confidence. She had grown up as an only child in a family circle where she was the center of love and attention, and it showed. But she was also as strong-headed as I was.

This was a combination sure to cause fireworks. Erika was a very warm and loving individual and she was puzzled by my aloofness and remote nature. Now that I have been married to her for over fifty years, I understand that long-ago problem much better. But at that time I was devastated. Here I had made a solemn commitment to genuine love, and I could not even get along with the one person in the world who loved me! It didn't matter whose fault it was, I felt that I should have been able to master this situation. After all, hadn't I been able to master everything else in my life? And hadn't I had an enlightening experience that had given me a deep understanding of life? At one time it appeared that we had parted for good, and since I assumed that my lack of emotional sensitivity was to blame, I allowed my emotions free reign and went into a deep depression.

Meanwhile I continued to work on my self-improvement by discovering more faults that needed correction. My mystical experience had increased my trust in Jesus' teachings, and I thought of his words from Luke 18, "for the proud will be humbled, but the humble will be honored." I decided to try humbling myself, thinking that this was the way to overcome my cockiness. You can imagine what happened next. I became a victim of the reality I had created by focusing only upon what was wrong with me. I had the mistaken notion that being as diligent as possible in finding and correcting my faults would lead to self-improvement. I found more and more faults with the result that I systematically undermined my self-confidence.

I also remembered the training method in the military. First, we had been deliberately humbled and degraded to eradicate "unmilitary" behavior. After that, we had been built up again to be good soldiers. I had gone through this process and had become a good soldier. So I adopted this method now to become the person I wanted to be. However I had failed to realize that I needed to depend on myself to rebuild my confidence, and I could not do that very well after I had torn myself down. I had "thrown the baby out with the bath water." I don't recommend this method of self-improvement to anyone.

I was studying physics at Humboldt University at that

time and was supported by a grant from the City of Berlin. The University was located in East Berlin which was controlled by the Soviets, and I lived in West Berlin's American sector. I had had difficulty gaining acceptance to the University because the Eastern Communist Regime favored applicants from labor and farming backgrounds. At first I had no problem commuting to the eastern sector. However in 1948, West Germany, in cooperation with the Western Allies, introduced a new monetary currency in West Berlin, and suddenly my grant was reduced by 90%, because it was being administered in East Berlin where the official currency was still the old one.

The political split between East and West continued to escalate. In June 1948, Stalin shut down all surface traffic between West Berlin and West Germany. Berlin became an isolated island in Soviet East Germany. Stalin had started the blockade to subjugate West Berlin to the Soviet system. The Allies responded with an unprecedented and heroic airlift that rescued West Berlin from the Soviets.

The citizens of West Berlin were experiencing great want, but they stood united against oppression, led by their resourceful and beloved Lord-Mayor Ernst Reuter. Electricity was available only one hour during the day and one hour after midnight. In the winter I had one tablespoon of coal dust per day to stay warm. I remember sitting in my ice-cold room trying to stay warm in a sleeping bag while writing my term paper. Black flakes from my makeshift carbide lamp gently settled on my paper, and when I wiped them off, they left large black streaks. The blockade lasted until September 30, 1949, one week after my marriage to Erika. My love for Erika was a key factor that kept me going. She had the courage and the faith to marry me against all obstacles.

A few years later I was an experienced professional design engineer with patents and technical publications to my name.   A major U.S. corporation offered me an attractive position, and our young family, which now included two little girls, crossed the Atlantic on the first cruise of our lives – all expenses paid, at a time when the U.S.A. was severely restricting immigration from Germany.

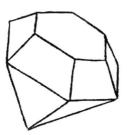

PART 4

EXPERIENCING

MULTI-DIMENSIONAL

REALITY

Chapter 11

Two Different Views

How do we get a better grasp of multi-dimensional reality? We live in it, yet we are only vaguely aware of it. Multi-dimensional reality is more significant than our physical world, according to **HP5**, yet it does not appear real to us. We understand why this is so. The dimensions of human consciousness are too limited. However this should not stop us from researching multi-dimensional reality. We have researched physical reality and our scientists have revealed much valuable knowledge about the physical world. Formerly, technological capabilities such as flying or long distance communication were considered impossible. Now they are normal activities in our lives. Many now consider multi-dimensional activities impossible, such as telepathy, holistic healing, or life after death. Yet, the time has come to open our minds to this new frontier of exploration. Not that this is really a new frontier. These experiences are as old as the human race, but for a few centuries, society chose to pursue a different course. This pursuit gave us air travel, television, antibiotics, and computer technology. It also gave us the atomic bomb, biological warfare, and global terrorism. The human race gained control over physical matter, but in the process lost control over psychological and spiritual matters. It does not have to be this way. We can enjoy the benefits of technology **and** gain peace and harmony in our lives.

We must understand the laws of multi-dimensionality in addition to the laws of physical nature. We need a science of multi-dimensionality, indeed a science of spiritual reality.

One reason why scientists are reluctant to entertain such an idea is that multi-dimensional reality does not lend itself to the well-proven methods of scientific research. Multi-dimensional experiments do not yield clear-cut Yes/No answers in the same way that physical tests can. The German quantum physicist Werner Heisenberg formulated this fundamental principle in his famous Uncertainty Theorem (see Appendix). A three-dimensional observation simply does not yield all the information about a multi-dimensional event. The whole is invisible from the lower dimensional level of its parts (**HP3**). However, quantum physicists can make very accurate statements about a large number of similar events and thus can determine the probable outcome of such events quite accurately. The same approach should be taken in any multidimensional research. For instance, no single case in the studies of Dr. Stevenson and his team (Chapter 1) conclusively proves the existence of reincarnation. However, the thousands of case studies together support a very high probability of reincarnation. It would be scientifically negligent to ignore this information. If we take Dr. Zammit's studies into the afterlife, not any one observation may scientifically prove that life after death exists, but the sheer volume of reports sets the probability of life after death beyond reasonable doubt. The same can be said about the viability of receiving information from the multi-dimensional domain through channeling, in reference to Jon Klimo's extensive studies. Let us, therefore, examine what has been reported about multi-dimensional experience in the afterlife, using descriptions from individuals who survived such experiences, from channeled information, and from hypnotic sessions. Subsequently, we'll examine how multi-dimensional reality might be experienced from the highest possible multi-dimensional viewpoint.

THE DEATH EXPERIENCE

According to Holistic Logic, we are more alive after our physical deaths than we are now, because the whole is more real than its parts (**HP5**). After shedding the dimensional restrictions of our bodies, we are more exposed to multi-dimensional reality, therefore we are closer to life's source. Seth states, "In many ways, then, you are 'dead' now – and as dead as you will ever be." A wealth of information is available about the death experience. An Internet search for "life after death" produced over 52,000 references. Descriptions about the death experience are available through channeling and from people who died clinically, but who were physically revived and remembered their experience on the other side. Such events are called "Near Death Experience" (NDE). According to the International Association for Near-Death Studies, Inc. (IANDS), some 13 million adults had NDEs in the United States. Other organizations are also studying this subject.

In 1975, Dr. Raymond Moody Jr. published a book titled *"Life After Life,"* creating much interest in this subject. Many more NDE books have been published since. An individual's death experience depends on her mindset, as with any life experience. Nonetheless, NDE reports follow a certain pattern. "NDE experiencers," as they are called, described how they suddenly released from any pain and felt calm, peaceful, and assured. Many reported looking down on their own bodies lying on operating tables while doctors and nurses desperately tried to revive them. The patients sensed death by feeling disconnected from the activity they observed. In his book *Transformed by the Light*, Melvin Morse, M.D., quotes a Georgia housewife who 'died' after an auto accident.

> I no longer felt fear nor did I feel my body, for that matter. I could hear them working around me but it meant nothing.

After experiencing separation from their bodies, the dying found themselves traveling through a dark tunnel at extremely high speeds towards a bright white or golden light. The light is intense, but looking at it does not hurt. Most experienced this light as "magnetic" and loving. Others, who believed in hell, interpreted it as menacing. On the other side of the tunnel, the dying persons usually met family members and friends who had previously died. They also reported being helped by guides and a "being of light" who appeared to "glow." The latter may or may not represent a symbol of religious tradition. The "being of light" engaged the deceased in a life review. According to an Ohio lady from Dr. Morse's book,

> This Being of Light surrounded me and showed me my life. Everything you do is there for you to evaluate.

NDE experiencers gain great insight into what path to follow in their remaining years on Earth. Some individuals report being told that they have to go back in order to complete an unfinished task. Others chose to do so on their own because of obligations or loved ones they did not want to abandon. Usually, NDE experiencers felt comfortable and at home in this environment of light and love, and they were reluctant to return to physical life. However, in a few cases an NDE was frightening.

After returning to physical life, NDE patients tended to have great difficulty relating their experience to others. The multidimensional conditions on the "other side" simply do not fit into our limited thought patterns. This is particularly true for the concept of time. Individuals who have come back from an NDE were unable to say how long their event had lasted. They couldn't relate their experience to our time scale. Generally, the near death experience had a profound, life-changing effect on these individuals. Their whole outlook on life changed. NDE experiencers returned with a deep understanding that we are all one, and that a universal love connects us all. They now consider themselves more spiritual, often independent of religious teachings. None who experienced NDE fear death. NDEs have been reported throughout history and in different geographic locations. Researchers report the same NDE pattern for all people, regardless of cultural, educational, religious, and even atheistic backgrounds.

Reports about conditions after death are also provided by channelers and people under hypnosis. (Please note that the term "after" is meant in our terms. In multidimensional reality, everything is simultaneous). In her channeled book *Seth Speaks*, Jane Roberts devoted some 60 pages to the after-death experience. Michael Newton, Ph.D., reports in his book *Journey of Souls, Case Studies of Life Between Lives*, how he interviewed people by using age-regression hypnosis, leading them back through their childhoods, births, and then to their lives before birth.

Seth states that you are in the after-death environment while you sleep. Your dreams give you glimpses of your activity there. You do not understand their full meaning because information is lost in the translation to your waking consciousnesses. The dreams that you remember are fragments of what is a coherent flow that makes perfect sense in multi-dimensional reality. While you sleep, your multi-dimensional Self is active exploring various possibilities for your waking life, according to Seth. Therefore, you are advised to "sleep on it" when trying to make an important decision. From your higher Self's viewpoint, your physical self seems unreal, just as your dreams coming from multi-dimensional reality seem unreal to you now, according to *Seth Speaks* by Jane Roberts. Your higher Self, unrestricted by space, time and matter, has a far wider range of possibilities. For instance you can move anywhere simply by the power of thought. Thinking of a place puts you into that location, and thinking of a person results in a meeting with that person. Seth explains that this can be a startling surprise for people who have just died. After a few experiences of instantaneous travel, they learn to watch their thoughts more carefully, which is what anyone should do, dead or alive ☺. It is said that some individuals do not, at first, believe that they are dead because they feel so alive. Guides help them to adjust to their new condition, according to Seth.

Channelers, NDE patients, and individuals under hypnosis provide us with the following additional reports. The recently deceased are said to often be surprised of how real the multi-dimensional domain is. Initially, the new environment can be quite confusing, particularly for people who did not believe in life after death. It's reported that teachers and guides help them to become reoriented. Some new arrivals feel that this is really their home territory, they feel more comfortable in it than in physical life. According to the reports, the deceased pursue meaningful tasks. They have the opportunity to understand the lives that they had recently left. An advanced guide helps them to re-experience the past life from a multi-dimensional viewpoint. The reports inform us that this experience is not about punishment or torment, but that it is an opportunity to understand the effects of our thoughts and actions. The review takes no time because time does not exist in multi-dimensional reality.

The information gained from the life review helps us to plan our further evolution. Unlimited new experiences are then open to us, according to Seth. In Jane Roberts' books, he describes that we can choose how we want to evolve. Each individual situation is different, but generally we may pursue three main areas of activity, according to Seth. We may decide on a new incarnation, we may rework our past lives with a better understanding, or we may enter an altogether different system of reality. Jane Roberts writes that the latter option is only open to individuals who have completed their reincarnational cycle. This means they have developed their abilities as much as possible through reincarnation. Once we have committed ourselves to evolving though physical reincarnation, we must complete this cycle. Seth explains that we choose how long (in our concept of time) we want to experience and "relax" in multi-dimensional reality. Eventually, most of us will choose a new incarnation. We may decide what kind of experiences we want to have in our next life. Supposedly, we may choose our next parents, within certain guidelines discussed with our guides. According to Seth, we may literally create an outline of our upcoming physical life. Then, when we actually live it, we may follow our plan but we can also deviate from it. We always have free will, but we are obliged to live with the consequences of our decisions.

According to Neale Walsch's *Conversations with God*, your soul decides the time and circumstances of your birth and death. From your soul's perspective, death is the release from a confining environment that has served its purpose. Thus, death is good. From a multi-dimensional point of view, there is no such thing as an accidental death. The brick that falls on your head is pre-ordained to do this at some deep unconscious level of your soul. Your soul does not drop the brick, of course, but with its superior awareness it subtly guides you to the right place at the right time. You, of course, consider it the wrong place at the wrong time! Your ego does not understand this process, but your soul does. With its superior knowledge and perception, it knows what is best for you – the whole You.

SEEN FROM ABOVE

In the preceding section we reviewed descriptions of how individuals experience multi-dimensional reality in the afterlife. This experience, while free of the limitations of physical life, is reported to still be limited by the individual's mindset. Compared to an individual's experience, how could we possibly imagine the entirety of multi-dimensional reality? Picture yourself looking at the stars. You cannot fathom the vastness of the physical universe, yet even this is only a minute fraction of total reality. Most reality is invisible even to our best telescopes, because they detect only three-dimensional objects in our 3-D reality. The total reality has infinite dimensions, including infinite possible 3-D worlds.

Holistic Logic tells us of a hierarchy of holons, a "holarchy" with untold dimensional levels. The higher the level, the more encompassing are the scopes of consciousness of the entities that dwell there. Ultimately, All-Entity/God's consciousness encompasses everything. The consciousness of each human, animal, plant, and yes, inanimate object is part of the consciousness of God. You can imagine your consciousness as a subset of the God consciousness. As you travel down the holarchy, from the highest multi-dimensional level down to the smallest physical manifestation, consciousness appears progressively less developed until finally, you behold the consciousness that resides in the smallest particle, a cell, molecule, or electron. However, from the viewpoint of God – the ultimately True viewpoint - no separations and subdivisions exist. All is one (**HP2**). Only when viewed from a lower level does separation appear, not because it exists, but because the lower consciousness does not have enough dimensions to experience the unity of all. This is why there are so many different religions trying to explain the same reality.

So how does God view our world, if it appears unreal from His viewpoint? According to Hindu and Buddhist scriptures, as well as to *A Course in Miracles* and *Conversations with God*, our world appears as an illusion from the top of the holarchy. Then why does everything appear so real in our world if it is only an illusion? Why does it hurt when I stub my toe on a table leg, and why can't we walk through walls if they are just illusions? This is the great mystery, the great enigma of spiritual reality. How can something be an undivided whole where parts don't exist, yet simultaneously consist of separate parts that are so real at their own level? How can our world, consisting of oceans, mountains, trees, and the keyboard in front of me, be so real and yet an illusion from God's viewpoint – from the most significant viewpoint (**HP5**)? You already know the answer: Your conscious mind does not have enough dimensions to experience all that is. So you perceive only a fraction of reality and for you, that is all the reality there is. For you, that is the "most real" reality.

Seth tells us that we are hypnotized by our illusion. A hypnotized person can fully accept false suggestions from the hypnotist, while onlookers see the deception. People under hypnosis experience the hypnotist's suggestions as real. In the same manner, we experience what we believe. As a hypnotized person experiences pain when stubbing his toe on an imagined table leg, we experience our reality through our mindset. We think that we are awake, but we are not awake to the whole reality. We are obsessed with our imagined reality to the point that we exclude everything else.

Think of the entire electro-magnetic frequency spectrum. It ranges from the lowest radio waves through microwaves, light, X-rays, and up. We only see the light, a minute portion of the entire spectrum. Imagine what we are missing by not having X-ray eyes! If we could see the highest frequencies, our world would be mostly empty space with subatomic particles widely separated from each other like stars in the universe. We know this from physics. Material objects would no longer appear solid.

We cannot overemphasize the importance of the viewpoint. As long as our mindsets limit our consciousness, we literally perceive our own world as different from ultimate reality.

Calling our world an illusion does not imply that it does not exist. The illusion exists in its own right, like a shadow on the wall, as any aspect of the whole appears as a separate part when viewed from the part's lower dimensional level (**HP4**). It simply has a less significant reality than the Whole (**HP5**). The "real" reality is All-Entity/God. One of our most inhibiting core beliefs is that we are separate from God. **Believe that you and God are one, and you will become increasingly aware of it. Believe that this is true for everyone, and you will experience that we are all brothers and sisters.**

WHY THE ILLUSION?

Why do we have to go through all this trouble? Why can't we just be and enjoy ourselves as the integral parts of God we really are? Try to imagine how life would be if everyone and everything in the world were in utter harmony. There would be no opposites. Everything would fall into place for us automatically. We would never be challenged, and thus we would never become aware of our own potential. There would be no reason to do anything. Most of us would soon get tired of this type of existence. We all have a need to experience ourselves and to test our capabilities. There is a big difference between sensing our potentials versus implementing and experiencing them.

Suppose the holarchy of illusions did not exist. Suppose that nothing existed but All-Entity without Its parts. It wouldn't even make sense to call All-Entity a whole. The whole of what? There would be only this one entity, without inner differences and separations, according to **HP9**. And it would not be the highest entity either. The highest of what? This solitary Entity would have all attributes of All-Entity - it would be conscious, would have enormous power, and it would be vibrating with the force of life. This solitary Entity would have unlimited multi-dimensional potential. It would also be Love since It lacks any differences and separations. But It would have nothing to do because there would be nothing to interact with – a very trying condition for a conscious entity bursting with energy. What would this solitary Entity be conscious of? There would be nothing to perceive other than sensing Its own existence. Picture a person held indefinitely in a room that is totally white and empty, with no distinguishing features, not even visible corners. This procedure is said to have been used for torture. All-Entity, without the universe, would not be able to express Its unlimited multi-dimensional potential if there were nothing else to which It could express. This scenario is reminiscent of a pressure cooker ready to explode. Perhaps this is the cause behind the big bang, the beginning of the universe (in our terms of time).

So we can imagine why All-Entity is motivated to create. This means All-Entity must create something that is different than Its own oneness. What is different from oneness?   Separation and multiplicity.   However All-Entity cannot create separation and multiplicity by dividing Itself. A division of All-Entity would destroy Its wholeness, which is the essence of All-Entity. All-Entity would cease to be Itself.

However, All-Entity wouldn't have ultimate intelligence if It could not resolve this dilemma. Instead of dividing Itself, All-Entity creates the illusion of separation and division by creating parts that have fewer dimensions than the whole (**HP1**). Because they have fewer dimensions, they do not perceive the whole (**HP3**), and they think and act as if they were separated and divided (**HP4**). The parts can now coexist with the whole without the whole losing its oneness. Now All-Entity is no longer solitary. It has an unlimited field of activity in which It can unfold Its infinite potential. It can grow, and evolve. Now All-Entity experiences Its potential as "objects" in lower-dimensional space, as a sculptor experiences his creativity though his creations and thus develops even more creativity.

How does this scenario appear from the parts' view? They perceive each other without seeing the whole (**HP3**). So they experience opposites and they are challenged by them. In other words, they experience that which All-Entity was not able to experience as a solitary entity: separation and multiplicity. And, since the whole is immanent in its parts (**HP7**), All-Entity can now experience, through its parts, Its own opposite: separation and division. This means an expansion of the grandest consciousness there is. All-Entity remains aware of Its own integrity as a Whole, yet It also experiences Its myriad aspects from the viewpoints of its seemingly separated parts. What a magnificent experience!

Thus the primary Holon is created. The big bang heralds the birth of the Cosmic Holon. All-Entity (God) explodes in a cataclysm of creation. The universe, the stars, prehistoric man, modern man, dinosaurs, cells, and electrons are all created in the everlasting NOW. Yet God remains whole in multi-dimensional reality even as His many creatures appear separate in our eyes. The only way that God can create is by giving the illusion of dividing Himself into parts. He cannot create anything outside Himself because then He would not be All-Entity. Nothing can exist outside All-Entity, because All-Entity is the Whole of all that is.

The consciousness of the parts does not perceive the whole. The Whole exists, but the consciousness of each part has "forgotten" the Whole's dimensions. Therefore the part perceives only a differentiated world while in truth, it is still united in God. In other words, the part sees an illusion.

God experiences His potential by living through the experience of each one of His parts. Each one of us represents an aspect of All-Entity and each one of our experiences is an aspect of All-Entity's experience. We all have a need to actualize ourselves through our actions and through our interactions with the rest of the world. If we cannot act and interact in some way, we might as well not exist. This is Shakespeare's ultimate question, "to be or not to be." We as parts have no problem experiencing ourselves through action and interaction. There are many individuals around with whom to interact and plenty of challenging differences. God has this opportunity only through His parts, through us.

We fulfill God's purpose by being different than God, by having fewer dimensions of awareness. The "fall of man" was part of the divine plan. God derives His experiences through His parts. We all derive our experiences through interaction with our environment. An Olympic Gold Medal winner experiences herself as being better athletically than the other contenders. Most people experience themselves as decent human beings in contrast to the September 11 terrorists. You experience your own identity in comparison to those of everyone else. Ultimately, we all would like to experience ourselves as the aspects of God that we are. There is a big difference between knowing that you are a part of God, versus having a vivid experience of it.

Neale Walsch devoted many pages to this subject in his *Conversations with God.* According to this channeled information, we must experience physical reality before we are able to experience our oneness with God. Walsch writes that this is the purpose of the physical universe with its system of duality and opposites. It makes us forget our unity with God, and only after having experienced the presumed separation can we experience the exultation and magnificence of being one with God. We must compare one condition with the other. Without that comparison, we would not experience the difference, and therefore we would not experience our awareness of being one with God. Every experience works the same way. If we feel good, we are aware of this only because we have felt worse some time before. Or, as Walsch writes, if you consider yourself tall, it is only in comparison with others who are shorter.

A spoiled child appreciates its good fortune only after it has experienced adversity. If we experience nothing but the best, we don't experience it as the best. We have to go through the bad in order to appreciate the good. The spoiled child does not experience life as good because it takes its fortunate circumstances for granted. We are all exposed to the adversities of physical existence to grow beyond them and remember our true identities, our innermost Being – All-Entity. In reality, both God's and our experiences are the same, they are simply seen from different dimensional levels. The whole and its parts are one, when viewed from the dimensional level of the whole (HP2), and God experiences His own magnificence through the multitude of His parts.

Throughout this process, we never cease to be an aspect of God. However we have forgotten our real identity, by design, so that we can experience the whole glorious truth when we remember it. Without this cycle of knowing, through seeming separation back to Awakening, we would not be able to truly experience our ultimate essence, and neither would God, because we are all One.

This scenario provides a different interpretation of "original sin." In Genesis, God expelled Adam and Eve from Paradise because Adam had eaten a fruit from the tree of knowledge of good and evil. However, from God's viewpoint, this was a necessary evolutionary step, and therefore not sinful. It only appears sinful when viewed from our lower dimensional level because we don't see the whole picture. In reality, All-Entity does not punish.

From a Holistic Logic point of view, this interpretation makes sense. God is driven to create. He must create to experience His potential. If He did not, He would be like anyone who is blessed with abundant capability but never uses it. By living in our illusion, we are helping God to experience self-realization. And since we are one with

God, we are helping ourselves to experience self-realization. We are united with Him in a common task, pulling together, because we are all in it together. There is a continuous give-and-take between the whole and its parts. Any part's change corresponds to a change in the whole, and a whole's change corresponds to a change of its parts (**HP8**). The whole cannot experience life without its parts and vice versa.

Notice also how this ingenious system cannot possibly fail. If you experience an event that you'd call a failure, you now see that it is a necessary step towards self-realization. You could not experience your own essence before having first experienced something else. You do not realize that your soul, with its superior wisdom, guides you through adverse experiences to prepare you for the ultimate Awakening.

Chapter 12

The Challenge

WHY PAIN AND SUFFERING?

Most of us create much of our own reality unconsciously. While an infinite number of probable events exist in multi-dimensional reality ready to be implemented physically, we automatically tune into the ones that resonate with our beliefs, including the ones we do not remember or perhaps purposely ignore. Thus we create our joys and triumphs - and our pains and sufferings. Some will find it difficult to accept this idea. After all, who in his right mind would create pain for himself? Who in his right mind indeed? Are we sure that our minds are right? Are we sure that all our thoughts are joyous, loving, accepting, blessing, and grateful? Until we are fully aware of everything in our minds, we do not know this. We do not know what our minds attract.

Fear helps to create what we are afraid of. This is the multi-dimensional law of association at work: like attracts like. You may carry a long-held grudge and wonder why you are ill. In his book *Peace, Love & Healing,* Dr. Bernie Siegel writes of a woman who was close to death with cancer. Her condition changed dramatically when "her much hated husband suddenly died, whereupon she completely recovered."

Ultimately, the "right mind" is one with God. People living in this state of mind do not suffer. Feeling oneness with everyone else, they automatically "do onto others as they want others to do onto them." They are one with the others, so it becomes a matter of self-interest. Self-interest is "morally correct" when you identify with the whole.   Here is another formula for moral behavior: do what is in the whole's best interest.   This is also in your best interest, because your true Self is the immanent whole.   Identifying with the whole fosters Awakening.

Holistic Logic helps you to understand how you create pain in your life and how you can experience joy instead. All-Entity, the whole of everything, is in ultimate harmony and immanent in you.   Any thought or act that separates you from any part of All-Entity automatically separates you from All-Entity Itself.   You cannot be one with All-Entity and leave something out, because All-Entity includes everything.   Then you separate yourself from your own inner core, your source of life and harmony, because All-Entity is immanent in you.   You disengage from your very source.   It can feel like hell, and actually it IS hell.   Hell is separation from your own inner being, which is God.   The antidote is to forgive and love all of God's parts, including yourself.

Not all painful experiences are caused by what you may have "done wrong."   Your soul evolves through the experiences of its parts, the incarnated selves mentioned earlier.   In Jane Robert's *Seth Speaks*, Session 580, Seth explains that illness and suffering are not caused by God. Rather they are by-products of our evolutionary development, caused by our misdirected energy.   Through suffering we learn what not to do.   In this sense, suffering fosters growth.   Jane Roberts wrote, "Suffering is not good for the soul, unless it teaches you how to stop suffering.   That is its purpose."   Seth also states in Jane Roberts' *The Individual and the Nature of Mass Events*, that every illness serves a psychic or psychological purpose.   Modern medicine is beginning to address the effect of the mind on the body's health.   John E. Sarno, M.D. writes in his book, *Healing Back Pain – The Mind-Body Connection*, "Neck, shoulder and back pain syndromes are not mechanical problems. They have to do with people's feelings, their personalities and the vicissitudes of life." Dr. Sarno also mentions that many physicians consider ulcers to be caused by psychological stress. Paradoxically, ulcers are usually treated with medical, rather than psychological means.

Many other conditions may cause illness, according to Seth. The soul level of your inner consciousness may arrange for you to become ill for any number of reasons. Illnesses are often life-transforming experiences. A good friend of ours has overcome cancer. She is convinced that her belief in and her practice of the methods recommended by Seth saved her life. This experience transformed her outlook on life and may well have been the purpose of her illness.   An Illness can be quite symptomatic for a specific situation in your life. If you have a "pain in your neck," there may be a person with whom you are in conflict. Leg pains may indicate an unwillingness to move ahead. An illness may also save you from a much more serious calamity by keeping you away from danger. In hindsight, you may marvel about this lucky coincidence. Nothing occurs by chance from a multi-dimensional view, according to channeled messages.

But what about the suffering that is clearly beyond an individual's control, such as major disasters, earthquakes, epidemics and wars? Multi-dimensional laws apply to groups, families, cities, nations, and humankind, just as they do to individuals. The composite mindset of the individuals involved creates the reality for that group. Holon Principles apply to all entities, at all levels, according to Chapter 3. The whole and its parts are one, when viewed from the dimensional level of the whole (**HP2**). Each person's mindset determines the degree to which the mass event affects that person.   Someone involved in a major disaster may even gain from it. A homebuilder can well gain from a hurricane. Jane Roberts published an entire book on group experiences, titled *The Individual And The Nature of Mass Events, A Seth Book.* Seth explains that individuals participate in major disasters for their own reasons. People living on California's St. Andreas Fault or in the Mississippi River flood region made this choice, consciously or unconsciously.

Why would anyone choose such an experience? There could be many reasons. The soul's agenda is to grow through experience, and hard times may accomplish this more easily than good ones. For some people, the sense of excitement and adventure might be appealing, like roller coaster rides in an amusement park, or a scary movie. Others may want the challenge of rising to the occasion, becoming heroes under stress. People have various motives for various life choices.

Does the fact that people choose their own experiences relieve us of the responsibility of helping them? What of the poor people in flooded Bangladesh, or the thousands of children starving to death in Africa? Is it their own problem if they have chosen this fate? Of course not. People can be so mired in misery that their minds cannot rise above it. Their plight is self-perpetuating exactly because their minds know nothing else. If we accept the suffering of others, we accept it for ourselves, and we will experience it too, since we are all One. Whatever occurs to people anywhere in the world occurs in our own psyche, because the whole of all people is immanent in us. As events occur in our psyche, we share responsibility for them. We cannot pretend that it is none of our business. Multi-dimensional reality knows no separation.

Understanding pain is a natural byproduct of life on Earth. How do you deal with it? First remember that you create your pain, for whatever reason. Though you may not know why, the act of owning up to it puts you in the driver's seat. Claiming responsibility gives you power over pain. You stop being a victim. Do not fight your pain. You want to heal it, but fighting it makes it more real for you. As we discussed earlier, the more you actively resist a situation, the more you strengthens it.

Picture a holon. The pain is one of your experiences, one of your "parts." You transcend it as the whole that you are. With this viewpoint, you can accept your pain much better than if you would fight it and thus put yourself on an even level with it. You can even love your pain and find that you can live with it more easily. Loving it might actually eliminate its cause.

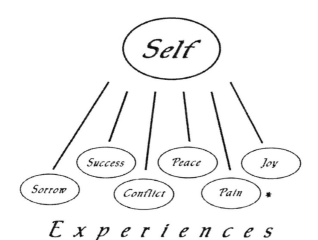

Figure 4.1. Experience holon.

Pain is an experience of how you feel versus how you would like to feel. In other words, pain is a separation between two states of mind. However no separation exists in All-Entity. Therefore, pain disappears automatically as you experience oneness with All-Entity. The closer to God we feel, the less pain we experience. It is such a simple truth, yet, how often do we actually heed it? Therefore, let pain remind you of your oneness with God.

GOOD AND EVIL

Why does evil exist in our world? Why does God allow it? Why don't we experience His total love and harmony? We already know the answer: Good and evil are part of the great illusion. Without evil we would not know what is good. Without pain we would not know joy. Without rejection or indifference we would not know love. Without the experience of the illusion, we could never experience the glory of All-Entity and our own participation in it. In the preceding section you saw that the purpose of pain is to learn how to avoid it. The same goes for evil. You avoid it by thinking and acting in harmony with the whole, which means with Love. Thus you awaken to the realization of your essence: being an integral part of God.

That which you consider to be evil has its purpose. Every evil you encounter challenges you to take a stand. It causes you to clarify and restate your own beliefs. The imperfection of this world challenges you to find perfection, to seek higher ground. This is the engine that powers evolution: the pressure of imperfection. Without it, you would not even know the goodness within yourself which is your true immanent nature. Consider how people opened their hearts and showed their compassion for the World Trade Center attack victims.

Without the duality of good and evil, you would never experience the indescribable joy of being one with God.

In fact, this is why you are here. You would not need to be born were it not for the experience of sorting out what is ultimately "good" and rising above what is not. Please remember the importance of your point of view. For you, as a part, "good" is what harmonizes with the Whole - All-Entity or God. From All-Entity's viewpoint, anything is a viable part of It, including what we call evil. Nothing exists outside All-Entity, otherwise All-Entity would not be the Entity of All. From an American viewpoint, the World Trade Center attack is one of the most evil deeds imaginable.   From God's viewpoint, it might be considered a necessary step for our spiritual growth, a mandate to ask and find answers to life's basic questions. From the multi-dimensional viewpoint, the death of 3,000 victims is their transition to a more harmonious and pleasant environment. It all depends on the point of view.

COPING WITH GLOBAL REALITY

Holistic Logic and its implications may appear daunting to you if you have never entertained the possibility of other dimensions. This is because your belief system paints a picture that differs from reality. To make room for more insights, you must set aside that which you think you already know. This can mean giving up long-held erroneous concepts. Just because everyone else holds those beliefs does not make them right. This was well demonstrated by the persecution of Galileo when he claimed that the Earth orbits the Sun. Or take the experience of the Dutch physicist Christian Huygens in the 1600's. He demonstrated experimentally that light travels in waves. However the scientific community rejected his opinion for an entire century.

Michael Crichton mentions other cases of scientific prejudice in a postscript to his book *Travels*. For instance, geology experts rejected Alfred Wegener's theory of continental drift for forty years until it was finally accepted.   Also, hypnotism was discredited for more than two hundred years. Crichton cites Max Planck, Nobel Prize winner in physics: "A new scientific truth does not triumph by convincing its opponents and making them see the light, but rather because its opponents eventually die, and a new generation grows up that is familiar with it."   We have ample evidence that our society has much to learn. Readjusting our common sense is not only well justified, it is mandatory.

With practice, holistic thinking becomes habitual. You'll develop a holistic common sense, and once you have it, you'll never let it go. Then you'll understand the causes of events better and you'll know how to cope with them. We are like travelers trying to explore the world by using our local map. Holistic Logic guides us into the unknown. As it turns out, the unknown is in our hearts, and opening our hearts is a matter of common sense – the new, holistic common sense.

How will this help us to face global reality? How does Holistic Logic deal with a horrific disaster like the September 11 World Trade Center attack? The answer is multifold because it was a multi-dimensional event. From the physical images seen by billions of people, through the emotions of the many thousands directly involved, the attack had a profound impact on the whole human race. True to the nature of multi-dimensionality, the perception of the event is different at each level. If we can look beyond the immediate profound pain and outrage and if we can grasp the global significance of this event, then we may see the hidden good that can come of it.

Let's distinguish between the three holistic levels involved in the WTC event: individuals, societies, and

Humankind-Entity.   Starting with the individuals, each one of them created his own reality.   This may seem preposterous, considering that thousands of people lost their lives, and tens of thousands were left grieving for their loved ones, not to mention those who lost jobs and the economic distress that ensued.   However, we do not see the whole picture.   On the soul level, individuals have reasons to end their lives, and others may expose themselves to loss so as to foster their spiritual growth. With their sacrifices, they have significantly contributed to Humankind's spiritual growth, and this may well have been their noble unconscious motivation.   This event has brought us together as none other, and being brought together is what we need in order to understand that we are all One.

Human mass events are created through the collective mindset of the individual people involved.   Individuals unconsciously choose mass events to foster their own evolution.   Each person has his own specific reason – perhaps to learn to cope with adversity, to make a statement of his choice, or even to conclude his present life.   Individuals make this decision on the soul level. From the soul's viewpoint, failure does not exist.   Every experience is a gain, no matter how we see it from our viewpoint.   Therefore we should not criticize others nor berate ourselves for what we perceive as failures.

After the attack, we heard the word "evil" hurled back and forth.   Evil does not exist from the viewpoint of All-Entity.   Everything occurs for a purpose.   The terrorists used terror because they knew of no other way to stop what *they* considered evil.   Western culture with its relentless power was penetrating their way of life.   Terror had become the strategy of the underdog.   It started with guerilla warfare and now it is used on a worldwide scale. Yes, terrorists are grossly misguided, but we would misjudge their motivation if we think that all of them are driven merely by their pleasure to do evil, as some commentators claim.   We would overlook their grievances and thus miss the cause behind this disaster. This is a mistake often made by the powerful.   Many terrorists are fanatic idealists for their causes, sacrificing their lives for their beliefs. They are heroes to those they represent. This does not excuse their deed, but it explains it.

This brings us to the second holistic level, the two main society-entities involved.   In this case, the conflict is between the ways of the Western, predominantly Judeo-Christian world, and the Arabic/Islamic world.   Most citizens of the West were surprised at the hatred expressed against them by those in Arab countries.   Most Americans hold no grudge against foreigners and their countries.   America is an open society that accepts peoples from the whole world, including Arabs and Muslims.   Americans wonder, "Why would anyone hate us?" This lack of understanding about the mentality of other people is characteristic of the disconnect between societies.   We must see that most decisions by Western political and corporate leaders were guided by self-interest, with little understanding and compassion for the Arab/Muslim world.   This is how our society works.   As long as we let "survival of the fittest" rule, we have to live with the consequences.   We create our reality, collectively as well as individually.

In addition to those factors, consider the vast discrepancy in living standards between the West and most Arabic/Islamic populations.   The appalling discrepancy between the two countries involved in the post September 11 war, America and Afghanistan, is quite symbolic for the nature of this conflict.   Physical conditions are symbolic for the underlying psychic, multi-dimensional reality.

Western tourists traveling though non-Western countries are shocked by the number of destitute people who have to fight loosing battles for survival. How do we think these people feel about Americans? Do they feel sorry that America lost a couple of symbols of its economic dominance, and that a few thousand Americans died in one incident? **Tens of thousands die of starvation *every day* in the rest of the world**. And does it surprise us that underprivileged people envy Americans for their wealth and influence?

The World Trade Center attack was a wake-up call for Western society and it is time to understand how these problems develop. Resentments have arisen throughout history, starting with the crusades in the eleventh century, and are now grievously aggravated by the Arab/Israeli conflict. As resentments accumulate over time, they eventually blow up in society just as they do in individuals, whether or not they are justified. Then it almost doesn't matter who represents society's grievances. If it had not been Osama bin Laden, then it would have been someone else. The longer the resentment is allowed to fester, the more irrational the blow-up finally seems.

The third holistic level of the WTC disaster is Humankind-Entity. Many channeled messages tell us that humanity as a whole is now entering a new evolutionary phase. The Internet SpiritWeb site (www.spiritweb.org) published several relevant channelings immediately after the WTC attack (Diandra, Sara Lyara Estes, and others). The multi-dimensional observers describing this event reminded us that we have all lived many lives throughout the eons of human evolution. During these lifetimes we have accumulated a store of thoughts and actions which are not in harmony with the whole of Humankind-Entity. In other words, unresolved issues have accumulated, primarily from the most recent centuries of human evolution, according to the channeled messages. Those issues must be resolved before Humanity ascends to its next evolutionary phase. This is apparently occurring now on a global level within a relatively short period of time. The issues that accumulated over eons are now compressed into powerful events experienced by all humans simultaneously, and by Humankind-Entity as a whole. Thus we are forced to recognize them as global issues.

While this is can be terrifying, it is nevertheless a healthy process. We are all being purified by this experience, because each one of us must face the issues involved and we must work them out together. The effect on Humankind-Entity is akin to a person seeing a psychiatrist and working through a set of inner conflicts. Each one of us is taking a position in the face of these events, and in doing so, we clarify where we stand. This is actually a great opportunity to find ourselves and to choose a higher form of being. There are no villains and no victims when looking from higher reality. We are making a necessary transition to a higher life form. The individuals involved performed a necessary function, and from a multi-dimensional viewpoint, bin Laden furthered this process. It is the old story of the "devil" doing God's work. Bin Laden and his helpers almost certainly do not know that they performed this function, and their mindset will create their own personal experiences corresponding to their deeds, but they probably sensed the importance of their mission.

How do you deal with this situation as an individual? It depends on the reality level with which you want to identify. By choosing, you clarify your position and the reality you experience. Now is decision time for the people of the world. We live in a crucial moment of world history, and the collective decision of the people determines humanity's future.

The best decision that anyone can make is to be the most highly evolved Self imaginable, thus creating the best reality imaginable. Thus you help create humankind's best reality imaginable. Any change in a part corresponds to a change in the whole (**HP8**), and in a multi-dimensional whole, a change of any part affects all other parts, (**HP10**). When making this choice, remember to choose LOVE – no matter what the appearance. True, America's leaders were compelled to use force against the terrorists. We couldn't allow anyone to mass-murder thousands of people. However, no amount of bombing and fighting will remove the underlying cause of this conflict. On the contrary, force will cause it to escalate.

To counteract this process, we should use our new understanding and send unconditional love to our adversaries. Regardless of what they have done, they are still part of Humankind-Entity and thus one with us. They need to be healed with love. If we give love, we will receive it - perhaps not from those who hate us so much that they are willing to give their life - but our love for them weakens their resolve and negative power. We are all connected in multi-dimensional reality.

Some of you may wrestle with your adverse feelings and opinions, because you are accustomed to thinking that honor requires retribution. The Love I am talking about here **is** retribution. This love is not the same as romantic love. I am referring to your innermost force. By sending this Love to your enemies, you draw upon God within. You do not have to be "nice" to the terrorists, but you combat hatred with Love. Love is the antidote for hate. Love is the last thing the terrorists want to see from Americans. It would prove them wrong and would turn world opinion against them.

After my initial shock at the WTC attack, I meditated and then did what I just recommended. At first I was not sure whether I could do this, but by tuning into God's Love, I was able to send genuine and unconditional love to the terrorists. I had the newspaper in front of me that pictured the nineteen assailants. I focused on each, one at a time. My action felt effective, as if it had hit the target. I also sensed that it widened my own spiritual scope. When we love our enemies, we do nothing less than identify with God, because God is unconditional Love. Then we are "in good company" indeed, and in the process we become more aware of our true identity - God within. We are Awakening.

Chapter 13

The Solution

THE NEW COMMON SENSE

Humankind creates its own reality through its collective mindset. The attitudes and beliefs of all humans collectively form the mindset of Humankind-Entity. Presently, humankind's mindset is full of contradictions. We want peace, love and abundance, yet we fight and hate each other and we destroy our natural resources. With its present mindset, humanity faces an unhappy future. Neale Walsch's Conversations Book 3, states that violence does not lead to a life of peace, joy, and love, that smoking known carcinogens and habitual consumption of alcohol does not result in good health. Also, exposing children to graphic violence on television does not help them to be good citizens. That same passage reminds us that it is foolish to squander the Earth's resources as if they are unlimited, and that the religious teachings of a punishing god do not help people to unite them with God.

Our ego-bound mindset prevents us from seeing this clear and simple logic. We must develop a new common sense. But our problem goes deeper and we are all contributing to it. Our beliefs do not portray true reality and thus we do not experience reality as it is. This is like viewing shadows on a wall and thinking that they are the real things, rather than recognizing the objects that cause them. We create our space/time reality because we believe in it. Yet from an elevated viewpoint, this is an illusion.

You experience what is in your mind, and it takes changing your mind to experience the truth. You must accept what is real regardless of appearances. Then you will experience reality. This differs from what scientists have told us. They have said that you must observe the "objective" world out there, and that from these observations you can decide what is true. Ironically, this approach has now led scientists to understand that reality is a non-material quantum field that is totally different from what you see. Now quantum physicists even say that consciousness affects what they perceive through their experiments. So science is approaching a concept of reality that corresponds to Holistic Logic.

Therefore, for humanity's sake, we should change our minds. This may look like an enormous and futile task, however we have four major factors going for us. First, humankind appears to be "sitting on the edge," and a gentle push from either side can send it one way or the other. We are in a state of transition, not unlike puberty. In this unsteady phase, relatively small influences can trigger profound changes.

Secondly, a groundswell of positive thought and meditation is already underway among highly motivated people who understand our situation and communicate with each other. The news media pay no attention to this activity, yet it is a powerful force, combining the dedication and conviction of those involved. This effort affects humankind's immanent inclination because of **Holon Principle 10**.

And thirdly, multi-dimensional Truth is already in our hearts. Thus we are "susceptible" to it and may accept it more easily than we think.

Finally, there is evidence that benevolent multi-dimensional sources are helping us through this critical evolutionary phase. Credible messages from the multi-dimensional domain have recently increased, judging by the number of channeled books being published (see the Bibliography at the end of this book).

In any case, we have no choice but to do our best, no matter what the odds are. Ultimately we can be empowered by the understanding that we create our own individual reality with our mindsets, no matter what happens to those who want to travel a different path. We won't necessarily be sharing the same future. We can start changing humanity's course by correcting our common sense. This is not the first time that such a thing has occurred in our history. When people believed that the world was flat, that conception was very real for them and a trip around the world was totally inconceivable. Now we perceive our Earth as three-dimensional, but a trip into multi-dimensional reality may fly against your common sense. It is time to change your common sense, to adopt a new, corrected common sense. Once you become accustomed to this new way of thinking, you will consider your old ideas as naive, just as we now consider belief in a flat world naive.

Let's look at ten ways in which your common sense can evolve.

OLD: We are separated beings.
NEW: We are all One.

OLD: We are separated from God.
NEW: We are one with God.

OLD: We live in 3-D space and time.
NEW: We live in multi-dimensional reality.

OLD: We are subject to fate.
NEW: We create our reality.

OLD: Matter is the primary substance of the universe.
NEW: Thought is the primary substance of the universe.

OLD: Death is the end of life.
NEW: Death is a transition to an expanded reality.

OLD: We are judged after death.
NEW: We will be helped after death.

OLD: Survival of the fittest.
NEW: Cooperation.

OLD: Man is nature's master.
NEW: Man is nature's steward.

OLD: Fight settles conflict.
NEW: Love settles conflict.

If we understand these tenets with our hearts, we will benefit from them. Holistic Logic must be assimilated intuitively as one cohesive whole, in order to apply it successfully. Employing a Holon Principle without consideration of the others can lead to contradictions due to their multi-dimensional nature.

AWAKENING

Understanding multi-dimensional reality is important because it is immanent in each one of us. If you want to be happy, you must be in harmony with yourself and the world.   And since multi-dimensional reality is the immanent essence of yourself and the world, you must be in harmony with multi-dimensional reality. It is simple logic. The immanent Whole of multi-dimensional reality is All-Entity/God. Nothing separates you from God but your misconceptions, your illusions about reality and yourself.   It is possible to put all these aside and experience All-Entity directly, even while living in a physical body. This is the ultimate multi-dimensional communion, called salvation in Christian theology, nirvana in Buddhism, and Awakening in the New Age movement.   From an elevated level of consciousness you'll experience your oneness with the essence of the universe. Then you'll realize that you have lived your life in an illusion of your own making.   You'll witness yourself like an actor in a play. You'll perform on stage for the experience of it, but you'll still be aware of who you really are. On the stage of real life, you don't need to follow a rigid script. You can change your plans as you go.

Like an actor, the Awakened mind knows its true identity while participating in this stage show. Thus you can be at peace in the middle of turmoil, enjoy your challenges, and love your life no matter how undesirable it may appear to others. Some religions call this heaven. Heaven is a state of mind, not a place. You do not need to die before you can enjoy it.

A century ago, Richard Maurice Bucke, a Canadian physician and a friend of Walt Whitman's, studied what we now call Awakening or Enlightenment. He described this in his book *Cosmic Consciousness*. Dr. Bucke was Professor of Mental and Nervous Diseases at Western University (London, Ontario). In 1888 he was elected President of the Psychological Section of the British Medical Association, and in 1890 President of the

American Medico-Psychological Association. The *Proceedings and Transactions of the Royal Society of Canada* describe how Dr. Bucke experienced "Illumination" while on a visit to England. According to the report, Dr. Bucke suddenly felt enfolded by a "flame-colored" cloud, which he at first mistook as a reflection from some disaster in the vicinity. Then he realized that the light came from within himself. This was accompanied by a sensation of great exultation and mental illumination that was impossible for him to describe. This experience is said to have left Dr. Bucke with an after-taste of Heaven for the rest of his life.

Dr. Bucke studied the Awakening experience from a professional psychologist's viewpoint. In his book he discussed fourteen historical personalities with highly advanced Awakened minds. In addition, he investigated thirty-six other personalities he considered remarkable but less developed. The first group includes Gautama Buddha, Jesus Christ, the Apostle Paul, Mohammed, Dante, Francis Bacon, and Walt Whitman. The second group lists such names as Moses, Socrates, Spinoza, Swedenborg, and Emerson. Bucke observed that evidence of 'cosmic consciousness' was becoming more frequent throughout the world, and he believed that humankind was approaching an evolutionary phase of higher consciousness. You can see this evidence today in the increase of channeled information.

When in harmony with the essence of life, the Awakened person attains personal traits that we all cherish, such as:

Effectiveness of spontaneous decisions.
Greater energy, alertness and self-confidence.
Inner calm, balance and emotional stability.
Freedom from time pressure.

So how do you become Awakened? Holistic Logic answers this as follows: remember that you create your own reality through your mindset. Whatever you believe, you'll experience as your reality. Therefore, to Awaken, you must want to believe in it. You want to believe that you are already one with All-Entity/God. How fast your beliefs create your experience depends on the clarity of your beliefs, their strength, and your freedom from distracting thoughts. To 'remember' your oneness with All-Entity, you should dwell on the conviction that this oneness already exists here and now, regardless of appearances. This works because your innermost Self *is* Awake – only your ego keeps you from believing it, and your ego is not your true Self. In other words, you do not have to do anything to achieve union with All-Entity. Striving is counter-productive because this presumes that the union does not yet exist, which is not true. This belief prevents you from experiencing the union.

All of your life you have been told that you have to strive and work hard to reach your goals. Now you know otherwise. You reach a goal by making it real in your mind as vividly as possible, visualizing it with all its desired aspects and consequences. Then you state it in concise language, which sharpens your mental focus and brings it closer to physical reality. Thereafter you'll act accordingly, intuitively, and much more effectively.

If your goal is to Awaken, how can you apply visualization when you cannot visualize All-Entity? Your physically oriented mindset cannot visualize your union with All-Entity/God (**HP3**). However, God resides in you, in fact, He IS You, your innermost You. So it's just a matter of letting go of your limiting beliefs. You must literally change your mind about reality and yourself. Since you already have the Truth within you, you must jog your mind to its inner core, to remember your true essence.

How do we jog our minds to remember? We let go of interfering thoughts and think of things that are closely related to what we want to recall. In other words, we use thought association. If we want to remember what we had for lunch last Tuesday, we recall what we did before, during, and after lunch. Then, when we remember who we were with, where we were, etc., we can more easily picture what was on our plates.

Your approach to Awakening works in a similar way. Sit quietly in a meditative state and let go of your thoughts. Then try to "remember" God within you. To jog your memory, you can think of some characteristics of God. You may use those mentioned in Neale Walsch's *Conversations*: God is totally joyful, totally loving, totally accepting, totally blessing, and totally grateful. Identify with these. Say them aloud if possible, I am totally joyful, etc. Then be completely still. Just sit there and be. Any of your other thoughts have fewer dimensions than God and interfere with experiencing oneness with God. Let go. Try this twice every day. When you sense love in your inner core, hold on to it and know that it is God. Dwell on it. It is beautiful! This Love is totally joyful, totally accepting, totally blessing, and totally grateful. This Love is different from the emotion of affection and attachment you may feel toward one person but not another. Divine Love is all-inclusive, and it is powerful. With Divine Love you can even love your enemy without being submissive.

In Glenda Green's book, *Love Without End, Jesus Speaks ...,* we learn why we should love our enemies. This loving has nothing in common with passive submission, the acceptance of suffering, or with being a "nice guy." Rather, when we love our enemies, we have no choice but to draw on the Divine Love within ourselves. There is no outside reason to love. This is an opportunity to identify directly with God.

Hold the feeling of Divine Love that you sensed in your meditation and carry it with you as you pursue your activities. In other words, implement unconditional love in your life. You can start practicing with those closest to you, purifying your thoughts until you feel nothing but heartfelt love. Remember that this love should be unconditional, so forgive any lapses and think of every soul's perfection. Do this consciously every day. Does this mean that you must do everything the other person expects of you? No, it doesn't. It does mean, however, that you'll think and do that which results in the highest good for all, including yourself. Love will tell you what this is.

Eventually, you'll include more and more people in this web of love, your friends, neighbors, and acquaintances. If you think that people must be lovable before you can love them, please reconsider this belief. You have an immanent supply of Love which is infinite and unconditional, so it's simply a matter of finding it within yourself. In this way you'll identify with God and you'll Awaken to your union with God. If you expect love in return, your love is not unconditional. As you become more loving towards others, those others will become more loving towards you. You will find that love will become second nature, requiring no effort on your part.

With time, you'll be able to love even your enemies, even those you once considered despicable, like Adolf Hitler and Osama bin Laden.   If you think that such people are unworthy of your love, please think again. Your immanent store of love is infinite and unconditional, regardless of what others may do.   All-Entity/God includes everyone and everything unconditionally. If you don't do the same, you do not identify with God and delay your Awakening.

Our enemies, personal and collective, perform a necessary function, as we discovered in Chapter 11 (Why the Illusion?). Without them we would not experience the illusion of imperfection that is necessary to appreciate the state of perfection. It is necessary in order to experience Awakening to the union with God.   It is in our self-interest to forgive our enemies and to love them - unconditionally.   Granted, this may seem to be a tall order, but it only appears so this way because we do not see actual reality.   Channeled messengers advise us repeatedly not to judge others.   They say that we shouldn't criticize them because we don't understand why they are the way they are.   Jesus' most important instructions were to love God with all your heart, all your soul, and all your mind, and to love your neighbors, and your enemies. You may have thought this meant that God would then reward you for good behavior. Instead, Jesus gave humankind a recipe for Awakening based on eternal multi-dimensional laws. There will be no judgment day, just holistic reality, a loving and logical process.

For those who feel uncomfortable with these ideas, you may be relieved to know that our holistic guidelines are **not** commandments. You are completely free to do whatever you want. Some may want to rebel and do the opposite, thus experiencing the opposite of the Whole within. Thus they experience separation from their own inner source and may create a "living hell" for themselves. But no one can drop out of All-Entity's all-encompassing embrace. Eventually, these individuals will have had enough of the misery and will come "home," because, in reality, they were never separated.

If you think of yourself as a sinner, then you are emphasizing your sense of separation from God and are hindering your Awakening. Yes, we all have our score of wrongdoing, but if we want to Awaken we must forgive ourselves and others and learn to identify with our innermost core. This core is beyond reproach. Some may consider it blasphemous to say that we are the same as God. But how can we feel one with God if we consider ourselves not qualified? All-Entity accepts all of us, It IS all of us, it is the Whole of All-That-Is.

You cannot offend God, because God is one with us. Can you offend yourself? If you act in an offensive way, you are simply creating the illusion of separation for yourself. In other words, you deny yourself the limitless dimensions of All-Entity. Holistic Logic tells you that this is unwise if you prefer peace of mind, love, and joy.

There are many paths to Awakening. Some are based on Eastern religions and philosophies, such as Yoga, Vedanta, and Zen Buddhism. All aim at abandoning ego-consciousness and identifying with All-Entity/God. Some systems involve rigid disciplines. Channeled books from several authors (Mary Margaret Moore, Tom Carpenter, Neale Walsch) tell us that the shortest and easiest route is to totally accept that you already are one with God. In practice, there are as many approaches to Awakening as there are people in the world, because each person represents a different aspect of God and thus starts from a different viewpoint. It is of no benefit to fight with those who hold other religious views. Doing so emphasizes separation, the very thing religions should seek to overcome. The fully Awakened mind ignores the illusion of division. It doesn't even see dimensional levels, because none exist from God's viewpoint. From your earthbound viewpoint, dimensional levels do exist and they help you to understand cosmic reality, but eventually you will see them and the entire cosmos for what they really are: an illusion. All-Entity has no divisions.

The way to Awakening is to identify with the God within by letting go of your misconception of separation. There is nothing to pursue because you are already one with God. There is nothing to do other than to become aware of your true inner core and to let go of the illusion. At least once a day, be still. Let go of structured thought and open up to All-Entity where no structure exists.

Please understand that the Holistic Logic described in this book is a device to help you get oriented, to aid you in shaking off ingrown misconceptions. It can lead you to understand the concept of Awakening. However, it is not a path to Awakening because it is still structured thought. The Holon Principles are only aspects of multi-dimensional reality. This is true of any structured approach to ultimate Truth. All-Entity is not structured. It is not divided into separate aspects. It is an undivided One. As stated in Tom and Linda Carpenter's *Dialogue on Awakening*, Chapter 4, "the process of awakening is a concept of the ego. You are Awake! You are completely whole. You do not see it." It is your limited concept of yourself, in other words, your ego, that gives you the impression that something must be overcome. Separation is only an illusion: something to let go, not to overcome.

IS JESUS THE ONLY WAY?

> Jesus saith unto him, I am the way, and the truth, and the
> life: no one cometh unto the Father, but by me.

So it is written in the New Testament. The time when this
was written was between AD 50 and 150. Most of the
writers were not alive when Jesus lived. His stories have
been passed on verbally. The original text was in Greek
and was translated and reinterpreted many times
afterwards. We cannot be certain, therefore, about Jesus'
exact words and the context in which they were spoken.
According to Holistic Logic, no separation exists in All-
Entity, thus no soul is barred from God. It is
inconceivable that God would give preferential treatment
to one sector of humanity, leaving the rest in the lurch
because they happened to grow up in a different part of
the world. This is inconsistent with unconditional love.

Jesus was fully Awakened to his oneness with God.
he referred to this one-consciousness as "Christ." Jesus
probably spoke the above quoted statement in this frame
of mind, as Christ. Therefore his words would mean: no
one comes to God but by one-consciousness with God. In
other words, Awakening requires that you accept that you
are one with God. No problem here. This is **HP2**: the
whole and its parts are one, when viewed from the
dimensional level of the whole. Other world religions
express the same concept in one form or another.
Buddhists seek to experience nirvana, Hindus believe that
their inner Atman is Brahman, and Taoists seek their
mystical unity with Tao.

I am more comfortable with certain contemporary
channeled messages than with writings that have been
translated, reinterpreted, and revised many times over the

course of two millennia. I don't doubt their divine origin, but I am not sure whether the translations, reinterpretations, and revisions were equally divinely inspired. Tom & Linda Carpenter's *Dialogue on Awakening, Communion with Jesus*, emphasizes that we should not focus on the individuality of Jesus but on our oneness with God, which is Christ. For instance, page 117 states, "there is the Mind which expresses God which I have called the Christ." And on the next page: "the Truth that is embodied within the Christ is expressed through many and it is no different than the Truth which I express to Tom. I encourage you to look beyond the identification of any single expression of the Christ."

LOOKING BACK

When I look back upon life I see that it was a continual balancing act between living according to Holistic Logic and the practical demands of daily existence. After a euphoric experience of oneness with God, I dove into the mechanics of earthly life, seeking to make that experience permanent. I made a determined effort to eradicate my shortcomings and implement love in my daily life. However I soon found that this would have required a super human effort as I struggled to harmonize my spiritual aspiration with the demands I faced as a family man and breadwinner. I had a good job and our family enjoyed a good life, but I found it difficult to merge my spiritual goal with my professional life. I certainly could not discuss this problem at work in my scientific and technologically oriented environment, and as a result, I may have appeared reserved to my colleagues.

At home, our marriage and family life was warm and harmonious. Before we were married, Erika and I had made a sincere commitment to each other that has lasted throughout our lives. We considered marriage a challenge. We knew each other's individual habits and characteristics and we were aware of which ones might cause us difficulties, as several did in the early years. But we always trusted the other's honest intentions. Giving more than we received was the motivation of our love. Erika had given birth to another little girl a year after we had come to the USA. We were proud and happy to have all three, and I loved and cared for them with all my heart. My family was the "proving ground" for learning to love, as I had intended.

During this time, I never lost sight of my goal to Awaken. I meditated regularly and I kept adjusting my thinking as life confronted me with a variety of challenges. For a long time I was unsatisfied with my apparent lack of spiritual progress. Yet, in retrospect, I now realize how I must have changed. There was progress after all. As I write this book, I am assessing how far I have come in my quest. To my own surprise, I feel that I have virtually arrived. I say "virtually," because the outcome differs slightly from what I had expected. I thought that I would be able to perceive multi-dimensional reality directly. I can't. But when I count my blessings, I know that there is nothing more to want. I hope that you will be able to attain this same joyful state of mind.

Whenever I want, I can enjoy God's presence through God's deep Love within me. My heart wells up in joy, and as it opens, I feel at home with All That Is. It is a feeling of being in love, personal, mutual, and intimate, yet all-inclusive. Erika and I still share a bond of deep love, trust, and respect towards each other and towards our daughters. In addition, we enjoy a warm, closely-knit circle of friends. I have become much more compassionate, tolerant, accepting, and patient with others whom I would have scorned in the past. Remembering my own failings makes this easy. I enjoy peace of mind, without fear, including the fear of death. I feel that I am right at home where I am spiritually. Having revised my beliefs for decades, I have become sure about my priorities and this makes me feel comfortable with my decisions. I am healthy and full of joy again, much as I was when I was young. I am perhaps not quite as exuberant, but calmer, more self-assured and anchored internally.

Erika and I have been blessed with all that we need materially. Our happiness does not depend on more possessions and we are confident about the future. We like to travel and we have already seen much of the world. I recall life's basic questions that I asked as a young man,

What is life all about?
How should I live.
How can I come out on top?
What is the top?

I am satisfied that I have found my answers. I know that being completely Awakened means having a vastly more expanded consciousness than the one I have now. But I know that this is okay. I feel and know that I am one with God and that God is with me and all around me. I am where I want to be. A book titled *Mysticism*, by Evelyn Underhill, states that a profound spiritual experience is often the starting point for seeking spiritual Awakening. It appears that we are all participating in a cycle experiencing unity with God, then separation from God, and back again to unity, endlessly. This is the breath of God.

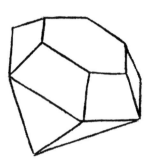

CONCLUSION

SUMMARY

Perhaps the most dramatic chapter in Humankind's evolution is occurring now, in our lifetimes! We are now breaking the mold of traditional limitations, allowing ourselves to venture into entire new directions. We are becoming aware of a domain that has countless more dimensions than our three-dimensional space. Historically, humans have always known about the invisible multi-dimensional reality and called it the spiritual realm. However that realm was beyond human understanding and only subject to religious beliefs. In the more recent past, scientific research of physical reality provided a rational understanding of the visible world and even led to a belief by many that the visible world is all there is. However now this same science has arrived at the limits of what can be understood in physical terms and is knocking at the gates of the great unknown invisible domain. It is becoming increasingly evident that that unknown domain is what we always called spiritual.

Spiritual reality has always been considered beyond rational understanding. However, we are now beginning to understand the spiritual world with our logical, rational minds. We are discovering that fundamental spiritual tenets from Vedic scriptures, Buddhism, and Christianity agree with this new logic. We will develop a new "technology" with this advanced understanding, and this technology will enable us to become true masters of our destinies and to maintain peace and harmony in the world.

Holistic Logic, the hidden logic of spiritual reality, will help you to understand the new direction of human evolution. This logic is based on observations we can all make in our environment. We can observe that everything in the universe is organized into wholes and their corresponding parts, from galaxies down to the smallest subatomic particles. We are all aware of this basic feature of reality. Although we take the existence of wholes and parts for granted, their mutual relationships have not yet been fully understood. A holistic analysis of these relationships opens the door to the "holy grail" of cosmic understanding. When we understand these relationships, we can see how they are consistent with the Theory of Relativity and the results of quantum physics research. Yet, we don't need to be scientists to understand Holistic Logic. The facts are right before our eyes, if we would only shed our loyalty to our preconceived ideas. All we have to do is to observe reality from a new perspective. Then we can understand multi-dimensional logic and discover that it is the logic of spiritual reality. This new Common Sense can make sense to all of us.

But to adopt the new perspective, we must abandon some erroneous notions. One of them is the idea that the "objective" world we perceive is independent of our own minds. Until recently, scientists took it for granted that there is an objective world "out there" that can be observed without being affected by the observer. Now, quantum physicists have concluded that this is not true. The objects we observe depend upon consciousness. The mindset determines what we see and experience. This idea is fundamental to Holistic Logic. It is the key to understanding physical *and* spiritual reality as a unified cosmic reality. Our points of view determine what we see and experience.

In this book we explored the whole and its parts, the basic building block of reality. We did this by carefully choosing our point of view. We switched our positions back and forth between the whole and its parts and observed that reality appeared changed depending upon which view we took. We looked at the same reality, but our changing viewpoint changed our perception of that reality. Thus we developed ten Holon Principles that, when taken together, make up Holistic Logic.

After we successfully tested Holistic Logic with practical examples, and after we judged it applicable to multi-dimensional reality, Holistic Logic led us to a number of important conclusions. For instance, we discovered that our collective viewpoint is the reason why we don't perceive the spiritual reality beyond our physical world. We also realized that our visible world is only a small part of a vastly larger cosmic reality, most of which we do not see. Our three-dimensional space is only a subset of unlimited dimensions.

The Holon Principles help us to understand that any whole has more dimensions than its corresponding parts. They also tell us that we cannot see the whole from the lower dimensional level of the parts. We cannot see the whole because at the parts' level we lack the dimensions necessary to perceive the whole. This is why we do not perceive multi-dimensional reality. And this is why quantum physicists see only either a particle or a wave instead of the combination of both, the quantum whole. This is also why we may not notice how our own mindsets determine our fates, and how we could control our fates by controlling what is in our minds.

Holistic Logic showed us how we hurt ourselves when we hurt others. It's an automatic process. Deep in our psyches we are united with everyone. When we alienate ourselves from others, we alienate ourselves from our own psyches. And our psyches are the inner source of our lives.

In the terminology of Holistic Logic, the whole of everything is All-Entity. All-Entity is the unifying Whole of the universe. Being the highest entity, we may call it God, but this God does not have the human characteristics often implied by religions. Since All-Entity embraces all that exists, It accepts all. In other words, All-Entity is unconditional Love, and unconditional Love accepts us as we are. Otherwise All-Entity would not be the entity of all. Divine rejection of sinners is a human concept, not a divine one.

Holistic Logic empowers us to rise above our present limitations. We cause our limitations by viewpoints that identify with separations and differences in our world, in other words, with the lower dimensional level of the parts. When we identify with the whole, we awaken to the multi-dimensional level of the whole and overcome our differences and conflicts.

Humankind is now wrestling to resolve the seemingly insurmountable differences between its parts.   The mindsets of many are so focused on differences that they cannot identify with the whole that unifies all. Thus they forego the peace and harmony of the whole. You, who have read this book, now know how to overcome these problems and how you can rise to the level of the whole to enjoy peace and harmony. And you know that with your own progress you help others to proceed as well. We are now in a critical phase of humankind's evolution. Its progress depends on the progress of individuals. Every one of us carries the shared responsibility of doing our best.   Every one of us has the opportunity to experience the most glorious experience of all, to be one with the All.

WHERE WE ARE NOW

The biggest problem we have as members of humankind is that we emphasize separation. Consideration for others is decreasing and violence is increasing. The behavior of children is a good barometer of society's psychological climate. Who would ever have dreamed of school children gunning down their teachers and classmates? Only an emotional disconnect from other people makes this possible. Individuals are moving away from the realization that we are all one and that the life source is within. They are moving away from peace, joy, and harmony. But we shouldn't blame the children. Adults are even worse. For decades, nations have developed terrible weapons of mass destruction – napalm, massive nuclear arsenals, poison gas, and biological weapons. Any one of these is capable of killing vast numbers of innocent people.

On the industrial front, powerful corporations exploit and deplete natural resources. The oil industry projects "optimistically" that the world's natural oil reserves will last about 40 years *at current rates of consumption*, according to Thom Hartman's book *The Last Hours of Ancient Sunlight*. Yet world oil consumption is rapidly increasing with the population growth and industrialization of Eastern countries. No adequate effort is being made to solve this problem. Imagine society running out of crude oil, our main energy source and the basis of vital products such as plastics! Can you picture the havoc in our world economy when oil prices skyrocket as oil reserves are exhausted? Don't believe that corporate leaders wouldn't let this happen! Our younger generations will have to face this crisis.

Another well known trend is global warming and the loss of the protective ozone layer. In a January 2001

United Nations conference in Shanghai, hundreds of scientists from around the world unanimously approved the final report that linked global warming to man-made pollutants. The report predicted widespread drought, floods, and violent storms caused by a rapid temperature increase. The Earth's average temperature could rise as much as 10.4 degrees in 100 years – the most rapid change in 10 millennia. Advanced computer models show that humankind is causing global warming. The models predict melting of the ice caps and the rise of sea levels up to 34 inches! The resulting floods will displace tens of millions of people in low-lying areas. Worldwide drought will lead to extended wildfires and will scorch farmlands, resulting in unprecedented famine. Another activity that directly threatens our survival is the unscrupulous elimination of the rain forests that produce the oxygen we all need to breathe. Thom Hartmann reports that 38 million acres are being destroyed every year. At this pace, rain forests will not survive in our children's lifetimes.

The gap between the rich and the poor has increased dramatically. ABCNEWS.com reported that the world's three richest families own more than the 43 poorest nations **combined** while tens of thousands of people die **every day** of starvation and related diseases. On the medical front, antibiotics are being used with careless abandon, for livestock as well as for humans. As a result, bacteria are being groomed that are increasingly immune to antibiotics.

Poor countries have an urgent need for advanced drugs to treat their suffering populations. Yet, drug companies prefer spending fortunes on research that will provide medication to treat wrinkles, impotence, baldness and obesity. The Parents Television Council reports that "filthy language, graphic sexual raunch and mindless violence on prime time TV has tripled in the last decade." The Council considers TV shows sleazy, violent and anti-family and feels that this influence will lead our nation's children "down a moral sewer." The list goes on and on: overpopulation, mass starvations, extinction of animal species, fish stock depletion from over-fishing, uncontrolled dissemination of nuclear material etc., etc.

The trend is clear and pervasive. We will continue down this road unless we make a conscious effort to change direction. We claim to be an advanced civilization because of our technological achievements, but we are spiritually under-developed. Humankind is like an immature teenager who is speeding down the highway without a driver's license. The root cause of society's unfortunate behavior is ignorance. If we could understand how we hurt ourselves as we hurt others in pursuit of our own advantage, we would think twice. The backlash occurs automatically through the hidden "mechanism" of multi-dimensional reality.

We do not see the whole reality so we do not see how we hurt ourselves. We do not see the inner connection between our actions and what we encounter later. I am not speaking of morals here; I *am* speaking of a definite cause-and-effect process that we do not recognize. This cause-and-effect is like any other law of nature. We may call it "supernatural," because we do not yet understand nature as a whole. Once we see the connection between our thoughts and actions and their consequences, we will avoid hurting others lest we hurt ourselves in the process. This is a matter of self-interest, like not wanting to touch a hot stove. The only difference in that example is that we get burned immediately so we derive an immediate understanding from the experience.

Our problem is a lack of understanding. Whenever we misunderstand a situation, we'll make mistakes. Eventually these mistakes accumulate to form a quagmire and we must do some soul searching. The time for soul-searching is NOW. In our society, individuals tend to blame others for their misfortunes. This is profitable for lawyers, but it does not address the original cause of mishaps. You create your own reality. If someone involves you in an auto accident, your subconscious mindset put you into the accident-prone situation. To eliminate your vulnerability, you must change your mindset. Anyone who continues to have problems in his life must eventually face the music and find the cause within himself, in his attitude and in the way he thinks. This also applies to humanity as a whole. We are at a turning point similar to the one when mankind realized that the world was not flat or that the Earth was not the center of the universe. Now the change is even more significant. We will realize that our entire physical universe is but a small part of a much vaster reality that we do not see. Nevertheless, we are all internally connected and intimately united with everything that exists, visible and invisible. Understanding this truth opens up vast horizons and dimensions.

If you think that life is not bad as it is and that you can't worry about problems that are too big to do anything about, please reconsider. During my childhood in Germany, before the war, people felt good about the progress of their country. They had survived a devastating inflation, the economy was humming again, unemployment was non-existent, and the country was starting on the road to being respected once again. Trains were running on time, and the government provided building material and professional assistance for needy people to build their own houses. If crime existed, we were not aware of it. It was safe for us children to come home after dark. We now know that some adults saw the dangers brewing in Hitler's regime. These individuals were either silenced or they felt that life was not bad as it was, and that they could not worry about problems that were too big to do anything about. We know what happened. This is not a political book, but we cannot accept behavior that endangers our society without suffering the consequences. This lesson was burned into my mind in 1945.

HOW TO CHANGE

Society can change for the better, just as an individual can, by changing its mindset, by changing its collective belief system to match true reality. This requires adopting a new common sense. You know how to change your society. You start with yourself. You can change your own mind about the true nature of reality. Take the time and effort to understand, to think about it often. This is important business. Read the books listed in the Bibliography and pass them on to others.

Then live your belief. Remember the New Common Sense and apply it to everyday life. Look at the flowers and sense how you and they are all parts of One. Lift your eyes up to the night sky and feel at one with the stars, because you are. Sense the love in your heart and know that it is God. Then spread this love around and experience being "in heaven." Carry this feeling with you as you go about your daily tasks.

Stand up for your beliefs and express them to others if you can do so tactfully. Discuss this book's contents with your friends. Americans are learning to talk about spiritual matters without hurting one another's feelings. Multi-dimensional reality is too important and too intriguing to ignore. Without trying to "convert" others, be conscious of your beliefs when the subject comes up. Above all, 'know thyself,' know your real, innermost You. Your conviction and the way you conduct your life will reverberate through humankind and pave the way for all.

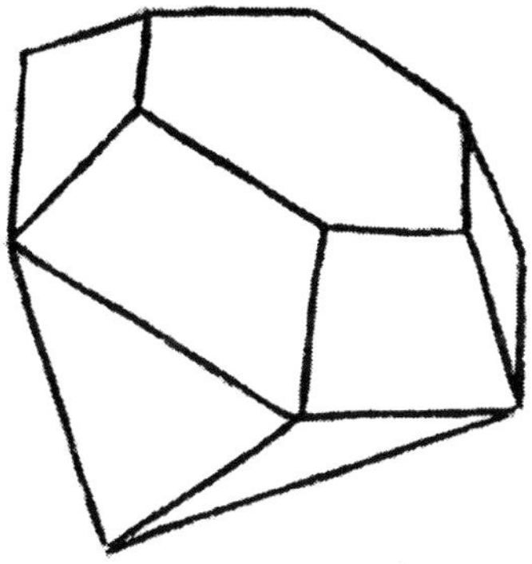

APPENDIX

SCIENTIFIC SUBJECTS

For readers who are interested in how Holistic Logic relates to modern science, this Attachment provides a number of relevant topics.

I. Energy - Mass

We discussed Albert Einstein's theory of relativity in Chapter 5. Einstein is also famous for his $E=mc^2$ formula. It states that the mass 'm' of a physical body times the speed of light squared is equivalent to a certain energy 'E' and vice versa. Mass, in our experience, has weight and inertia. Bodies that occupy space, such as billiard balls, have mass. In contrast, energy is invisible. We sense it only by its effects on physical objects, such as acceleration and heat. The fact that energy and mass are actually different versions of the same thing is difficult for us to visualize, although by now we have become accustomed to the idea.

Mass and energy are different aspects of the same whole that exists in multi-dimensional reality. As we experience an electron either as a particle or as a wave, so we experience the unified whole of mass and energy only as one or the other of its aspects. It is, again, like the 2D creatures seeing only circles or rods instead of the cylindrical pieces of nail (Chapter 1, Fig.1.4). The multidimensional whole of mass and energy is another good example of a holon. We perceive only the parts but not the whole – not because there is anything mysterious or unreal about the whole, but because our perception is limited to the dimensions of its parts.

II. Quantum Physics

Modern physics is based on Einstein's relativity theory and on quantum theory (also called quantum mechanics). Quantum theory was developed by famous physicists such as Heisenberg, Schroedinger, Bohr, and Dirac. While relativity theory focuses mainly on the macro world of outer space, quantum theory deals with the micro world of the atom and subatomic particles. Yet, relativity theory is also applicable to subatomic particles. As with relativity theory, quantum physics also assumes a multi-dimensional space in which our 3-D space and time are contained. The German Nobel laureate Max Planck initiated the evolution of quantum physics in 1900 when he discovered that energy consists of minute discrete portions, which he called quanta. We think of energy as a flowing medium, like water, but invisible. However, just as water actually consists of zillions of discrete molecules, energy is also divided into miniscule portions, except that they are much smaller, relatively speaking, than water molecules.

We have already encountered the quantum in Chapter 1 as a photon that appears either as a particle or as a wave. The photon is one type of quantum, an indivisible energy package. All quanta have the described particle/wave duality in our physical world, but they are undivided wholes in multi-dimensional reality. Electrons are quanta like photons, but their waves have a much higher frequency than light and therefore have much higher energy and mass. A quantum's energy is given by Max Planck's formula $E = h*u$, where h is a constant number, and u is the quantum wave's frequency.

Quantum Theory describes the inner workings of atoms mathematically, using many more dimensions than the three that we perceive in our physical world. Nuclear physicists routinely deal with hundreds of different dimensions with perfectly predictable physical results. Quantum theory is the basis of nuclear power plants, the atom bomb, and modern electronics.

The more we study our physical world, the more we learn that it is not as solid as we think. At the beginning of the 20th century, Ernest Rutherford concluded that an atom has a miniscule nucleus in the center and much smaller electrons orbiting around it. If we were to imagine a one-inch nucleus, then the whole atom would have a 1.6-mile diameter! In other words, those seemingly solid physical objects around us are virtually empty space.

Then researchers discovered that even these subatomic particles - nuclei and electrons - are not solid physical matter. Instead they are also composed of transcendent quanta with their dual wave/particle nature. The physical world that appears so solid to us is really a projection of invisible reality. Everything ultimately consists of invisible transcendent wholes and we see only their aspects as parts. **The deeper our scientists explore the nature of reality, the less physical and the more multi-dimensional it is.**

III. Double Slit Experiment

Holistic Logic provides a plausible explanation for the double-slit experiment that has puzzled quantum physicists. We will explain it here simply, referring to figure A1a. An electron gun shoots electrons towards a target screen. The arrangement is similar to a rifle practice range. Between the electron gun and the target screen is a shield that has two slits close to one another. We shoot only one electron at a time towards the slits. If we cover one slit, the target screen beyond shows a pattern corresponding to the slit's shape where the electrons have hit, as expected (l in figure A1b). The same thing happens if we cover the other slit (r in figure A1b). This means that the electrons behaved as we expected particles to behave.

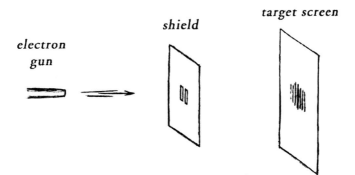

Figure A1a. Double slit experiment setup.

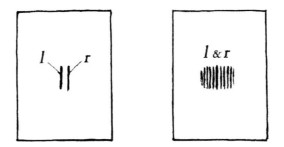

Figure A1b.   Target screen patterns.
l = left slit open; r = right slit open; l & r = both slits open.

However, if we leave both slits open, and we continue to shoot one electron at a time, the target screen shows a broad pattern of many lines (l & r in figure A1b) that spreads out to both sides much farther than the two former patterns l and r. Such a configuration is typical of interference between two waves that emanate from two slits. This means that now the electrons behave as waves.

We know that electrons can show up as particles or waves. The surprise is that in this case, only a single electron creates two waves. Since we shot only one electron at a time, there was no other electron to interfere. How can a single electron go through two separated slits simultaneously? It would be like shooting a billiard ball into two pockets simultaneously. The electrons showed distinct particle behavior previously when only one slit was open. Had they been waves then, they would have spread out much more to the sides, as waves do.

Holistic Logic's answer is that the electron is a multi-dimensional entity whose two aspect parts, particle and wave, appear in our 3-D space individually. Our viewpoint determines which of the two aspects we see. If we view the M-D electron through one slit, then we address the electron's particle aspect, and we see its particle behavior. However if we provide two slits, we address the spread-out character of its wave aspect. Therefore, we can view two different aspects of an electron by changing our point of view. The two aspects are always there, but because of our three-dimensional limitation, we can see only one at a time. How we look at it makes the difference.

We can say the same for all our experiences. We all look at the same basic multi-dimensional reality, but we each see different aspects, depending on our viewpoints.

IV. Heisenberg Uncertainty Theorem

In 1927, the German physicist Werner Heisenberg formulated his famous uncertainty principle, a cornerstone of quantum mechanics. This principle states that the position and the speed of a quantum cannot be measured at the same time. If we accurately measure the location of the quantum, we will not be able to determine its speed. On the other hand, if we measure the speed, we will not know where the quantum is.

We may also choose a compromise between these two extremes and get some information on both position and speed, but then both are fuzzy. Then the information is somewhat unreliable. Heisenberg determined the exact degree of uncertainty. The product of the two possible errors can never be smaller than a critical quantum factor "h" that Max Planck had determined in 1900.

Albert Einstein and other scientists felt uncomfortable with Heisenberg's conclusion. It did not satisfy the requirement of exact results to which physicists had become accustomed when making physical predictions and measurements. Yet Heisenberg proved without a doubt that this exactness does not apply to the quantum world. Repeated tests conclusively confirmed the uncertainty principle.

Holistic Logic suggests that this principle corresponds to a general holistic relationship between a whole and its parts. Returning to the cylindrical nail pieces mentioned in Chapter 1, let's photograph a larger cylinder (Fig. A2a). By taking pictures of it from various directions, we create different two-dimensional aspect views. In other words, we view a higher-dimensional object from the next lower dimensional order, using different viewpoints. Depending upon the relative position of the camera versus the cylinder, we obtain different aspect pictures as shown in figure A2.b.

You will notice that the cylinder can be seen as either a circle – when the camera on the far left is used, or a square – when the camera on the far right is used. Whenever we try to catch both aspects in one picture, the slanted perspective, as illustrated by the three inner camera positions, distorts each of the two head-on aspects. The limited dimensions of the observing device do not allow an undistorted picture of more than one aspect.

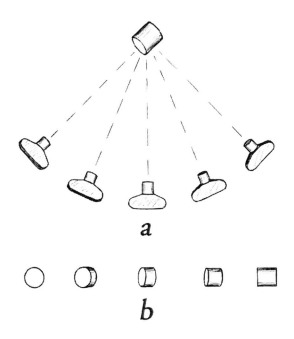

a

b

Figure A2.   Recording 2-D aspects of a cylinder.
  a.   Photographing from different aspect angles.
  b.   2-D images of different cylinder aspects.

We cannot simultaneously see more undistorted aspects of a whole than what the dimensional level of our perception allows. This is Heisenberg's uncertainty principle, expressed more generally in terms of Holistic Logic.

V. Holography

Holography is a method for making three-dimensional pictures, using two-dimensional photographic film. This technique was developed after the invention of laser technology. A laser creates "coherent" light of a single color frequency that travels as parallel waves, so that the light beam does not spread out, even over large distances. Coherent light is always required in order to create holographic images.

Figure A3 shows a typical holographic setup. A beam splitter (a semi-transparent mirror) separates a laser beam into two divergent beams, one horizontal and one vertical in our figure. Diffusing lenses spread both out into wider beams. This does not destroy the coherence of the light. The waves are slightly bent, but still virtually parallel.

A mirror reflects the lower, vertical beam in figure A3 onto a photosensitive plate, the holographic plate. This light beam now acts as a 'reference beam'. The horizontal beam passes through the beam splitter to a mirror, which reflects the beam onto the object to be holographed. The light that is reflected from the object hits the holographic plate. The two light beams, one from the object, the other directly from the laser, form an interference pattern on the holographic plate. The developed film shows swirling, interweaving circles that appear meaningless. That pattern is the holographic recording of the object.   It is totally different than the object itself.

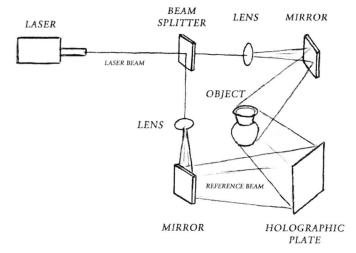

Figure A3.   Holographic setup.

However, if we illuminate the film with a laser beam similar to the reference beam used previously, we can observe the object, in our case a vase, as if it existed in three dimensions.   We can walk around the image and see it from different perspectives, just as we could see a vase. We could say that the three-dimensional vase is immanent in the two-dimensional holographic plate.

Another quality of the holograph is even more interesting.   If we break the plate into pieces, each one will produce a three-dimensional image of the object when illuminated with the reference beam, as the whole plate did.   Except now the definition of the image is not as clear as the one from the unbroken plate, but the entire object is visible.   A hologram is, of course, quite different from an ordinary photo.   When we tare up an ordinary photo, we can't see the whole object by looking at one piece.

David Bohm, the physicist mentioned before, referred to the holograph as a metaphor for how he envisioned the universe. Bohm felt that the holograph is a good analogy for his concept of an invisible "implicate order" and a visible "explicate order" that emerged from the implicate order. Bohm believed that each piece of the explicate order enfolds the implicate order, as each separated piece of the holographic plate enfolds the three-dimensional image.

About the same time in the 1960s, the Stanford neurophysiologist Karl Pribram had discovered that the brain does not store separate memories in specific portions of the brain, but that the whole brain recovers memories from what seems to be an invisible data bank. This finding also agrees with Holistic Logic in that Holistic Logic considers all events present in timeless multi-dimensional reality and that our inner self has conscious access to these events. Pribram adopted the holograph as a means to explain how each part of the brain can produce a memory of a past event, similar to the way that separate parts of a holograph can recover the object's image.

These two developments started discussions among proponents from scientific and religious circles, who hoped to arrive at a new worldview based on the holograph. In 1982, Ken Wilber edited a book titled *The Holographic Paradigm*, which presented the views of many highly qualified contributors. In 1991, Michael Talbot published *The Holographic Universe,* an excellent exploration of the unknown reality using the holographic metaphor as a guide.

However, the enthusiasm surrounding the possibility of finding a concept which could unify science and religion through the holographic principle has died down. Although the holograph demonstrates how the whole is contained in all its parts, in addition to a number of other interesting properties, it did not lead to a unifying theory.

As all analogies from our three-dimensional environment, the holograph conforms well to some, but not to all Holon Principles. The holograph is a good metaphor for **HP7** (The whole is immanent in each of its parts). Also, Holon Principles 1, 3, and 8 apply meaningfully, as a quick review will show:

HP1. The number of dimensions of the whole exceeds that of its parts. The vase image is three-dimensional while the parts of the holographic plate are only two-dimensional.

HP3. The whole is invisible from the lower dimensional level of its parts. We cannot see the image of the vase by just looking at the pieces of the holographic plate before it is illuminated with the reference beam.

HP8. A change in a part corresponds to a change in the whole, and a change in the whole corresponds to a change in its parts. If we would change the holographic pattern on that part of the holographic plate that we illuminate with the reference beam, the three-dimensional image of the vase would change as well. Also, if we change the object of which we take the holograph, the parts of the holographic plate would change correspondingly.

However the holograph does not demonstrate the remaining Holon Principles to any degree of satisfaction. For instance, **HP2** states that the whole and its parts are one, as seen from the dimensional level of the whole. It takes much imagination to see this relationship in the holograph. We cannot carry any three-dimensional analogy for multi-dimensionality too far. No three-dimensional analogy can demonstrate more than three dimensions. The best we can do is to use several different analogies that might highlight different aspects of multi-dimensional reality, all the while being aware of the viewpoint that we want to illustrate.

Rather than trying to consolidate science and spirituality with an analogy such as the holograph, it is better to identify the laws of reality that apply to both. **Holistic Logic unites science and spirituality.**

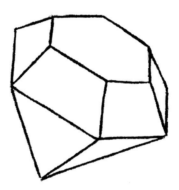

GLOSSARY

All-Entity	The integrated whole of everything that exists
Aspect	Partial exposure
Dimension	Extension in one direction
Entity	Autonomous unit
Group Entity	The transcendent whole of all group members
Holarchy	Hierarchy of holons
Holon	A whole and its parts considered simultaneously
Holon Principle	A logic relationship between a whole and its parts
Holistic	Relating to the organic whole of parts
Holistic Logic	The holistic whole of all Holon Principles
Humankind-Entity	The transcendent whole of all humans

Immanent	Inside and transcendent
Multi-dimensional	Having more dimensions than three
NDE	Near death experience
Part	One of several related units which together form a whole
Psyche	The non-physical part of a living being
Quantum	The multi-dimensional whole of a subatomic particle
Quantum Mechanics	Scientific theory of subatomic particles
Quantum Physics	Same as Quantum Mechanics
Self	The transcendent whole of body and mind
Spiritual	Same as multi-dimensional
Transcendent	Having more dimensions
Whole	Integrated unit of related parts

BIBLIOGRAPHY

The following books are recommended for further reading.

Bartholomew / Moore, Mary-Margaret, *I Come as a Brother, A Remembrance of Illusions*, 1985.

Briggs, J.P. & Peat, F.D, *Looking Glass Universe, The Emerging Science of Wholeness*, 1984.

Bucke, Richard Maurice M.D., *Cosmic Consciousness*, N.Y. 1901.

Capra, Fritjof, *The Turning Point, Science, Society, And the Rising Culture*, 1982.

Carpenter, Tom & Linda, *Dialogue on Awakening, Communion With Jesus*, 1992.

Chopra, Deepak, *The Seven Spiritual Laws of Success, A Practical Guide to the Fulfillment of Your Dreams*, 1994.

Cranston, S. & Williams, C., *Reincarnation*, 1984.

Davies, Paul, *God And the New Physics*, 1983.

De Quincey, *Radical Nature, Rediscovering the Soul of Matter*, 2002.

Dyer, Wayne W., *Your Sacred Self, Making The Decision To Be Free*, 1995.

Friedman, Norman, *Bridging Science And Spirit, Common Elements in David Bohm's Physics, The Perennial Philosophy and Seth*, 1990.

Gawain, Shakti, *Creative Visualization*. 1982.

Goswami, Amit, *The Self-Aware Universe, How Consciousness Creates The Material World*, 1993.

Gribbin, John, *In Search of Schroedinger's Cat, Quantum Physics and Reality*, 1984.

Hartmann, Thom, *The Last Hours of Ancient Sunlight, Waking Up to Personal and global Transformation*. 1998.

Hawking, Stephen W., *A Brief History of Time, From the Big Bang to Black Holes*, 1988.

Herbert, Nick, *Quantum Reality, Beyond the New Physics*, 1985.

Klimo, Jon, *Channeling, Investigation on Receiving Information From Paranormal Sources*, 1998.

Morse, Melvin. L. M.D. *Closer to the Light*, 1991.

Prabhavananda & Manchester, *The Upanishads, The Wisdom of Hindu Mystics*, 1948.

Roberts, Jane, *The Seth Material*, 1970.

Roberts, Jane, *The Nature of Personal Reality*, 1974.

Schucman, Helen, *A Course In Miracles*, 1992.

Sheldrake, Rupert, *A New Science of Life, The Hypothesis of Morphic Resonance*, 1981.

Siegel, Bernie S., *Peace, Love + Healing, BodyMind Communication & the Path to Self-Healing: An Exploration*, 1989.

Stevenson, Ian, *Children Who Remember Previous Lives*, 1987.

Talbot, Michael, *The Holographic Universe*, 1991.

Walsch, Neale D., *Conversations With God, an uncommon dialogue,* Books 1 – 3. 1995.

Watson, Lyall, Lifetide: *The Biology of the Unconscious*, 1979.

Wilber, Ken, *The Holographic Paradigm and Other Paradoxes, Exploring the Leading Edge of Science*, 1985.

Wolf, Fred Alan, *The Spiritual Universe, One Physicist's vision of Spirit, Soul, Matter, and Self.* 1996.

INDEX

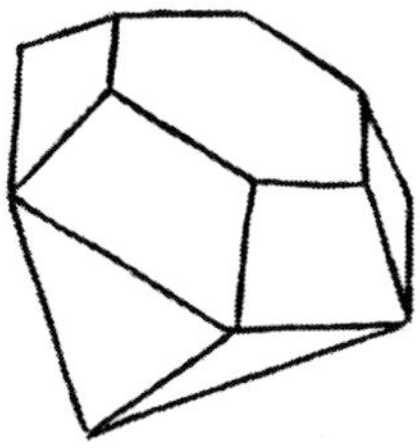

About the Author

    Joachim "Jo" Wolf was born in Berlin, Germany, in 1927. He studied physics in Berlin, followed by an electronics research and development career in Germany and the United States. He is now retired and lives with his wife in Southern Florida. Joachim Wolf's interest in metaphysics originated when he experienced a vision of higher reality as a young man. Attempts to describe this vision failed because it was beyond words. He then resolved to test his new understanding through experience, and to share his experiences and ideas with others later.

    In 1991, he wrote an essay, titled "Revolution in Common Sense." It describes higher reality through a comprehensive "Holistic Logic." In 1994, it was published on the Internet via CompuServe, and in 1996 as an Internet site titled "Quantum Metaphysics,"[1]. This site

---

[1] URL: http://home.sprynet.com/~jowolf

has earned a Key Resource award by Links2Go.com for being among the ten best sites to present metaphysics on the Internet. Numerous compliments and requests for more information have led the author to write this book. It describes his view of higher, "multi-dimensional", reality in more down-to-earth terms with many examples, visual aids, and practical applications.

ISBN 1553955567-6

9 781553 955672